American Honey

American Honey

A Field Guide to Resisting Temptation

Sarah M. Wells

RESOURCE *Publications* · Eugene, Oregon

AMERICAN HONEY
A Field Guide to Resisting Temptation

Resource Publications
An Imprint of Wipf and Stock Publishers
199 W. 8th Ave., Suite 3
Eugene, OR 97401
www.wipfandstock.com

PAPERBACK ISBN: 978-1-6667-3365-5
HARDCOVER ISBN: 978-1-6667-2849-1
EBOOK ISBN: 978-1-6667-2850-7

OCTOBER 14, 2021 9:04 AM

for Brandon

Contents

Acknowledgments

I AM GRATEFUL TO the editors and publishers who published earlier versions of the following essays:

"A Car to Drive," *Air: A Radio Anthology*

"Natural Habitat" and "Not-My-Husband," *Ascent*

"Genotype," *Hippocampus Magazine*

"Careful Intimacies" and "The Dance: Dad's Lead," *Full Grown People*

"The Worst Soccer Mom," *The Butter*

"Building Fires," *Rock & Sling*

"Someone's in the Kitchen," *Unfolded podcast*

"Field Guide to Resisting Temptation," *Brevity*

"Not-My-Husband" was listed as a notable essay in *Best American Essays* 2018.

"Field Guide to Resisting Temptation" was listed as a notable essay in *Best American Essays* 2014 and nominated for inclusion in the Pushcart anthology.

I am so grateful for my husband, Brandon, who believed in, encouraged, and trusted me to share the story of our first ten years of marriage, even and especially the hard parts. There is no one else I would rather walk through this world with than you.

Thank you to my three children who have been forgiving of their mother's laser focus on a computer screen over the years, which certainly contributed to this story being a comedy instead of a tragedy. So many thank yous to Lisa, Jillian, and Leeann, who were vital anchors in my life during challenging storms—you truly helped me keep my life together. My mom and dad have been unwavering in their love and support of me, and I'm forever grateful for the life they gave me.

Thank you to so many readers, teachers, and mentors who have helped shape the contents of these essays: all of the faculty members at Ashland

Acknowledgments

University's MFA Program, particularly Jill Christman, Steven Harvey, Kate Hopper, Sonya Huber, Dan Lehman, Joe Mackall, Robert Root, and Kathryn Winograd; Rachelle Gardner and Michael Miller for encouraging me to keep at it, and writer friends Marilyn Bousquin, Susanna Childress, Valerie Due, Tania Runyan, Ginny Taylor, and Addie Zierman who cheered on the writing, living, editing, and publishing process.

Grateful acknowledgement to the Ohio Arts Council for its support via the Individual Excellence Award.

Field Guide to Resisting Temptation

Do NOT SEND SONG lyrics to Facebook or post YouTube music videos or listen to any songs about love gone wrong or one night stands or anything on country music radio. Okay, no music at all. Tell him no more, you are done, you are disappearing, removing him from your phone and from your Facebook and from your email, and when you've said all that, mean it, don't re-add or spy or stalk. Don't search for him on Facebook again to see if he's posted any more YouTube music videos that you listen to and Google the lyrics of and then know he's still thinking about you late at night so that your finger itches the mouse and you almost click "Message," almost click "Poke," almost click "Add friend."

Whatever you do, don't send him a meaningless text or ask what he's doing or how things are going. When you think of something funny, text it to your husband. When something makes you angry or upset, text it to your husband. When you think of texting anything at all to anyone else, text it to your husband. When you want someone to tell you something beautiful and romantic and sexy and you can't get your husband to say it, text your best friend who knows what it's like to want to offer your heart, divided, just so part of it can be filled at least partway, and wait for it to pass. It'll pass. Just be still and wait. Don't call him. Don't text him. It'll pass.

And remember your kids, the ones that keep talking and talking, *Mom, Mom, Mama, Mommy, MOM!* but your thoughts keep slipping elsewhere. Remember them, strap them against your chest, wield them in your hands, stand them in front of your eyes, and eventually, you won't see through them anymore. Your three children won't understand your need for attention. Anything you do or say will shout that their dad wasn't enough. The same man you spent eight years creating babies with, for some reason isn't enough now, which isn't true, it isn't the full story, it's only a moment, this moment when you are small and insecure and not even looking for something more. They will wonder whether it was their fault. Later they will know it wasn't, it was you, all you. And him. And him.

Of course you will fail if you keep telling yourself he's just a friend, it's fun and easy, there aren't any consequences, you aren't actually doing something, just flirting, it's harmless, it makes you feel good, he's a city-a-state-a-country-an-ocean-a-universe away so what does it matter? What does it matter, except you wonder if it shows in your eyes when you tell your husband *I love you*. What does it matter, except you are afraid you might say something in your sleep even though nothing has happened, nothing is happening, nothing will happen. Stop lying to yourself. Turn off the computer. Put down your phone. Stop checking Facebook. Listen to your husband play the guitar and sing songs you adore. Eat your baked sweet potato fries and guacamole with a glass of American Honey over a game of rummy and realize later you are here, wholly, mercifully. Keep looking into your husband's eyes and search until yours answer.

I.

Rules of Engagement

"How can I ever surprise you with a ring if you think every date will lead to a proposal?!" Brandon asked. I was disappointed after every night out; I waited for it at Christmas, New Year's Eve, Valentine's Day, movies and concerts and dinner, my baptism at church, Good Friday and Easter, and still, no ring.

I didn't need a surprise. It was my last year of college, and I had no clear career prospects beyond my summer horticulture job at Six Flags Worlds of Adventure and "do some writing." I figured it didn't matter; we would get married, I'd have a baby, we'd start our huge and happy family, and maybe I'd keep writing while taking our beautiful and compliant children to soccer games and storytime at the library. We had been dating for *nine months already* and I was twenty. If we didn't get married soon, we might not ever.

At age twenty-five, Brandon had been through this twice before, with the same enemy, I mean ex-fiancée, who said *yes* and then *not yet* and then *yes* again and then *no*. She wanted him to be different than the man he was. He wanted her, but he didn't want to change. She kept that ring, that flashy, expensive ring he bought her, even after it was over.

I would inherit that debt, but I didn't care about money or whether or not we both had jobs or a place to live. I was in love, convinced that God had willed for us to be one. All I needed was a commitment to forever. Why was that so hard?

Brandon wanted to be *sure,* 100 percent positive that I was the One, the real and true and best threat to his freedom, before he entered into any future engagement. He wanted to be *sure* I would not demand his surrender, that I would not make him quit coaching or competing.

"This is who I am!" he said angrily in the car one night.

We learn our best war tactics from our parents. Brandon's never engaged in battle in front of him. Mine simmered and simmered and simmered

5

and then Dad exploded, then simmered again as if nothing ever happened. Mom waited out the silence, wondering if what happened only happened in her imagination, it had detonated and then vaporized so quickly.

In the car that night, I wept because we were fighting and he never fought, and the only way I knew how to fight was to retreat.

"Of course not," I said, batting my damp eyelashes, "I would never ask you to give up a part of yourself." I meant it, even as I swallowed the need back down into my gut, that need for someone to drop what they were doing and say, *You matter, you are a priority.*

Right then, all that mattered was getting him, keeping him, and I believed what I said: I would never ask him to change.

And yet that's the one and only certainty in this drive for vows: change. No parent bond, sibling rivalry, or best friendship comes close. Only a fool thinks neither one will change. I was already changing, navigating my life to line up with his, just as I had before with others. I would go anywhere, do everything, try anything to be with him.

As the sun set beyond the tree line in the Cuyahoga Valley and we drove from Macaroni Grille, I squeezed his hand and said, "This has been a really great day." My college graduation ceremony and bowtie noodles nestled warmly in my belly. There were even leftovers at my feet.

He took a turn and said, "Do you want to go for a walk?" and I said, sure, with a smile. One thing I knew about this man: he's an indoor guy. *Could this be it? Finally?*

We walked the shadowy boardwalk by the river, water raging below, highway racing above, branches low and full of leaves as if the entire world and its threats cocooned our relationship. We were two people choosing to love, two people pressing a force field out around ourselves. The darkness was interrupted by the occasional headlight and streetlight. He stopped in the shadows and knelt down on one knee, and I knew what he would ask before he did, so I said, *Yes,* finally, *Yes, yes, I will!*

I could hardly see the ring there in the shadows, but its stones caught rays of artificial light from the beams above, refracted and shimmered. It was beautiful.

It was beautiful, even after I discovered the receipt weeks later, after I bought a wedding dress and asked a few hundred people to come and witness our union. The crinkled paper I unfolded was not what I thought it might be—a receipt for our dinner on the eve of our engagement, a potential memento for our scrapbook project. No, it was from a department store, and I wished I had not found it.

I adored my ring; everyone eyed it. Everyone complimented it. I watched it shimmer in the sunlight, stared at it and considered its promises. *That is a beautiful ring!* They said, *I love your ring.* I smiled, *Thanks, I know.* I wished I hadn't opened the drawer. I wished I hadn't unfolded the receipt. I wished the final sale price didn't say what it did, that it was cheap, fake, a purchase and decision made in haste. I wished it didn't matter.

It didn't matter, because we were both broke and jobless. He spent so much time trying to figure out whether I was the one that he *must* have been serious, I reasoned, and anyway, I didn't care about material things. I liked flip-flops and tank tops. I didn't wear makeup. I forgot to wear gloves when I mulched at my summer landscaping job, and my co-workers scolded, "You're going to ruin your hands for your wedding pictures!" But this is who *I* am: strong, tough, confident, real. I want to feel my hands in the dirt. I want to build the callous where friction meets tenderness.

It didn't matter because he proposed, right? He wanted me, right? Even if the ring only cost a little over a hundred dollars, even if it seemed a hasty purchase . . . I remembered the ring he bought for his ex-fiancée, the ring she kept, but it didn't matter, none of it mattered. He asked me to marry him. Me. Me!

At a discount.

The war tactics I was taught engaged in my mind. *Just keep quiet, forget it. It's nothing. No one else has to know. It'll all blow over. Push it down, below the place where you keep your self-worth and bury it.* This gift was not insincere—he loved me and wanted me—and even as the rational mind negotiated facts the heart raced. *Is this all the sacrifice you are worth?*

Five years later, I would ask him to make the sacrifice I had promised against. A job opportunity presented itself and it looked fantastic. We sat down together at the dinner table with our infant daughter sleeping and our soon-to-be cranky son in utero, and I asked, "Are you willing to commit to being the stay-at-home parent? Are you sure you are willing to give up coaching and teaching? Will you have a problem with me being the primary breadwinner?"

He said, "Yes, let's do this." He said, "No, I don't care if you make all the money; I'll go golfing with the kids tucked into the back of a golf cart."

He had no notion of what was to come and neither did I, except that change is exciting and opportunity golden. I squeezed his hand and accepted a full-time job offer to serve as administrative director and managing editor at a university.

The new territory we possessed together was scattered with landmines and booby traps we had to navigate. He slammed doors and bought groceries and folded laundry. He yelled, "I hate my life!" I cried into pillows, "Why doesn't he just leave?" Later, we mocked each other's snappy retorts, "Aren't you going to get me some tea?" and "You don't matter," phrases we've each delivered in moments of stress and exhaustion. Soon they were just jabs and elbow nudges, as in, remember that time we really grated against each other? Remember the shrapnel, how it tore through the skin?

In the car before we were engaged, I told him, *No, I will never ask you to give up a part of yourself.*

Except one day in the future, I would find a part of myself and take possession of it. The treaty would be broken, revised, a new covenant written: *If you give up your dream, I will take this job, thinking that I'm doing it so you can go to seminary, so you can fulfill your calling, but instead I will have found mine. If you give up your dream, I will pursue mine and discover uncharted territory. If you give up your dream, I will become a different person, a more whole version of the woman you married.*

This was not what we signed up for but the rules seem to change along the way, no matter what we think or say—no, every ring is not authentic; no, sex does not just switch from a sin to a gift with the addition of vows; no, babies do not just happen, they are conceived and die in utero sometimes, in fact more often than I will be able to carry to term; and no, after that beautiful child arrives, I will not want to be a stay-at-home mom, after all, no, I want to work hard, I want to build the calluses where friction meets tenderness.

These are not the truths I thought I knew.

That's all so far down the path and into the jungle that it seems silly to even bring it up, except for all of those promises we were about to make, how I would never ask him to give up any part of himself, how all I wanted was to get married, *Come on, what are you waiting for, I want to commit my heart my mind my full energy my life my all to you right now, right now, and I'm tired of waiting.* Tired of waiting for someone to love me so much they're willing to stay with me forever, willing to walk with me, willing to build a life together.

With all of that, then, why was it such a big deal? Why did this ring and its price tag matter?

I waited for him to come, to find me in the national forest parking lot. The green leaves shook in the breeze, their rattling a dissonant scratch against the random roar of tires driving by on the road. A train whistle blew. Day hikers pulled into the gravel lot off Cuyahoga Street, slammed their doors and walked down into the valley and back up again. Still I waited. Battle tactics ricocheted in my brain, to speak or to scream or to sit silent, pretend that nothing happened, nothing was wrong, *you're fine, you're fine, it's fine.*

This was part of the commitment we were making, part of the promise I was already breaking, asking him to change. Asking him to make room in his world for me, a "me" whose identity was hardly formed apart from him, apart from any man, and yet there was a sparkle of it already. I mattered. This mattered. Speak.

When the words came they rushed like the flood waters in the Cuyahoga River. My hurt surfaced quickly and I waited, expecting his defense.

"I'm so sorry," he said. No excuses. No bitterness or blame.

"It's okay," I said. It's what I believed: This was not his fault but a fault of my personality, I should be stronger, I should care less about such things, they shouldn't matter, so this action, this hurt? It's okay.

"No, it's not okay," he whispered, "I made a mistake. I'm sorry. Please forgive me."

No, it's not okay.

I forgave him.

Ten years later, when I am still wearing that beautiful cubic zirconium ring along with an authenticated diamond wedding band from J.B. Robinson's, when we are still practicing for better, for worse, when I'm a more substantial and whole version of myself, my husband pulls me close after he's had a few drinks. He is a more substantial, whole version of himself, too, even intoxicated.

He pulls me close and whispers in my ear, or shouts it if we're out at a bar, "Someday, I'm going to get you a *real* ring," he says, serious, straight into my eyes.

I roll mine and smile, "Sure, someday."

I spin the cheap engagement ring around my finger. *That's a beautiful ring!* They say, *I love your ring!* They say. *Thank you,* I say with a smile. It *is* a beautiful ring.

Buck Owens Teaches Me about Listening

1.

"DAD, LOOK, HER HAIR grows," I said, curled in the corner of the home video with my new doll. I twisted her arm, the synthetic blonde hair loosed by a grinding mechanical crank.

"Dad, watch." I lowered her arm, the motor a slow rumble of hair tumbling from her scalp, like a time-lapsed video.

"Dad . . . " I said again.

Over the radio, Dolly Parton sang "Hard Candy Christmas," then Merle Haggard sang, "If We Make It through December," then Buck Owens sang, "Santa Looked a Lot Like Daddy." My dad made a very thin Santa. Across the living room, Dad stared at the bottom of a remote control car, screwdriver in hand, batteries in a slow roll off the coffee table. My brother hopped up and down next to his leg.

"Dad," I said again, "Watch." I pumped her arm again, the doll's straight arm chopping the air until the hair shrank back into her head. Buck Owens kept describing my daddy, Santa, over the airwaves.

"DA-AD!"

"What?"

2.

"Can I go with you?" I begged, and he nodded, jerking his head toward the truck.

"Let's go."

My wiry legs ran quickly to the truck. I pushed in the clear cassette mixtape of Buck Owens my aunts had made him and buckled. On my own radio in my bedroom, I listened to Faith Hill sing "Wild One" and sang

11

along at the top of my lungs. I was never a wild one, but he said the same thing in those quieter moments between jobs, maybe as I leaned against his leg or crawled onto his lap or nuzzled against him on the couch—*Sare*—I heard him say, *You can do anything you put your mind to.*

We drove to a job site where Dad would quote or measure, assess or invoice, meet with other men in jeans and Wolverine work boots. I hopped across the ruts left behind by the excavator as it rotated on its axis, reached its claw into the earth, pulled what was below above, and dumped the soil to the side. He did this every day, all day long, from seven in the morning until near dinner time, the roar of the semis and excavators and machinery slowly damaging his eardrums, the strain and rattle of equipment shaking his vertebrae until he needed four herniated disks removed, his calloused hands like bear paws, hardened and tough.

Earlier in the school year, on "Take Your Daughter to Work Day," Dad rolled up in front of the middle school in the Mack dump truck. The chrome-plated bulldog hood ornament glistened in the early-morning sun. I was glasses and braces, junior high gawky with thick bangs and a greasy ponytail who smiled too easily, but my dad drove a dump truck. He shifted levers and pressed petals and suddenly there was a pond, a basement, a driveway. He paved the way for my future. I stretched my leg as far up as I could and hoisted myself into the passenger seat, dropping my backpack full of books into the dirt of the cab. I hoped a boy was watching, the boy whose name I inscribed in cursive letters inside my notebooks with "Mrs." in front. The truck rumbled to life and groaned as Dad maneuvered the stick shift and clutch, and I buckled my belt, a whole day with Dad ahead.

On this summer day, he stood in sunlight, the sweat-stained brim of his hat low on his forehead, his eager daughter always eager to be with him skipping around the job site. He puffed casually on the cigarette as his lips moved. I didn't listen. I scaled the tracks to climb in the cab, bounced on the springy seat cushion, and crawled into the shadow of the bucket attached to the arm of the excavator.

"Sare!" he shouted, jerking his head and thumb toward the truck, and I pranced over the tracks in the mud. With one quick boost of muscle I hoisted myself into the passenger seat, swinging into the stifling air of the pickup.

"I'm thirsty," I said, running my tongue over the roof of my mouth. Dirt was in every crevice of the vinyl seat cushion and settled in clumps on the floor mats. Dad pushed the cigarette lighter in and tapped the pack against his palm until a smoke fell out, then clenched it between his lips.

"Can we stop for a drink?" I asked, working to find a cooler spot on the seat. He held the steering wheel with his hand, put the truck in reverse and looked over his shoulder, spinning the steering wheel with that leather palm until we turned off the lot and onto the road. I would practice this motion as a teenager, this one-handed turn, and feel the slow heat of skin against leather.

"Here, take a sip of this," he said, reaching toward the cup holder above the stick shift, handing me the can. The Miller Lite was sweating, too. I hesitated, then took a swig. It was cool but dissatisfying, burned, then sour. After taking a drink, my mouth was dryer. I gagged and put it back into the cup holder.

Dad chuckled. The lighter popped and he lit up, taking a draw from his cigarette, smoke slithering in ribbons as the window sucked it out and blew it back in, ashes flecking onto the headrest. I expected the smoke and the beer would kill him someday. I had seen the pictures of lung and liver cancer in health class. I paid attention. I turned toward my window and let the wind blow tendrils of hair away from my face. I tried to focus on each tree, each post, dizzy from all of the movement, as if we were stationary and the world in full motion. It hurt my eyes. I turned instead to my reflection in the rear-view mirror. I was so thirsty.

3.

We were somewhere in Death Valley; behind us, the McCarran International Airport rental lot in Las Vegas; ahead was Bakersfield. In 1998, all I wanted to do was call my boyfriend and cry about how much I missed him, how much I loved him, how much I couldn't wait to be with him again, but we were Out West for ten days, and I couldn't do that from the backseat of our rented minivan. Instead, while my dad drove and drove and drove, I wrote and wrote and wrote, until the Dramamine wore off and then I slept, sighing and pining over my Michael back home.

We made a giant figure-eight reminiscent of my father's trips Out West with his parents and six brothers and sisters, all riding with a cooler of Cokes and no A/C in a station wagon across the country. Instead of driving our way there, to save time, we had flown into Las Vegas and rented a van with a plan to shimmy up through California to see the sequoias, then cruise through Yosemite, back down to Vegas and out to the Grand Canyon, Hoover Dam, Bryce, Zion, and beyond.

Death Valley was hot and dry, the asphalt in front of us liquid waves radiating into thin air so there was no telling the division between earth and atmosphere. Dad liked to take the back ways places, even while he raced himself and the odometer to the next destination. Sometimes we drove rural roads, being passed by and passing no one, and wondered if we might dead-end at a cattle ranch. Somehow he always knew we'd come out on the other side.

We didn't go to Bakersfield to visit the thriving city whose population had expanded from 70,000 in 1970 to over 175,000 in the nineties. To us, Bakersfield was just a cowpoke Western town centered around Buck Owens and Dwight Yoakam, who both must've walked its streets. We parked at the Crystal Palace, the place Buck built two years earlier. I expected us to run into Buck. The walls were lined with his face and his records leading into an empty dance hall. It was the middle of the day. Music played over a central sound system. We went in and we went out, to find dinner and then to bed.

The rest of our trip, we hardly walked the streets of Bakersfield, hardly lingered near the hotel swimming pools, hardly toured more than the gift shops of the parks we stopped in for memorabilia that said We Were There, in our minivan. I begged Dad to stop at every scenic overlook, to walk into the wilderness instead of drive through it, but there was always more to see through the tinted glass of the rental, some destination beyond Here to reach before dusk.

On the day I turned sixteen, we drove and drove and drove, headed back out from Las Vegas to the Hoover Dam.

"Got any *dam* bait?" Dad asked, then laughed. My younger brothers giggled in the middle row of seats while I simmered in the back. It continued for what seemed like hours—"I'd like a *dam* map!" "How about a *dam* tour?" "There's no *dam* beer here!"—until I yelled from the back, "Can we stop with the *dam* jokes already??" All I wanted was for this trip to be over, to find a payphone, to cry into the receiver to my Michael, my future, ready to be married with babies in a house with a front porch and a horse and a cocker spaniel.

The day was early, the Dam still far in the distance, and Dad laughed, threw out a few more dam jokes, and drove, and drove, and drove.

4.

I wore a periwinkle blue high school band uniform and red feather plume, my hair tucked back in a French braid, black band shoes a little too tight, the elastic straps of my spats grass-stained after a long season. I had two red cords, one on each shoulder—I was a senior and a captain, a leader. I owned the term, "band dork." From my position on the gym floor at the end of football season, I scanned the bleachers. There was my Michael, a trumpeter who graduated in the spring, who would take me out later that night in his purple pickup with the lift kit and monster-truck wheels. There were the other parents, moms and dads staggered in gendered patterns, mom dad, dad mom, mom dad. And there was my mom, alone, video camera in hand, panning the risers and focusing in and out as I played my part as second-chair first clarinet.

We didn't play any Buck Owens hits in the band, of course. Even if we did, Dad wouldn't be sitting in the bleachers with the other parents wearing band parent t-shirts. Throughout the season, I would find him leaning on the fence by the home team end zone, watching from the sideline in the cool fall air. I knew he loved me. He would be standing in the shadows after the half-time shows, his strong arms tight around my shoulders, my band hat knocked crooked against his chest.

5.

The guys I dated were like my dad—hard working and good with their hands, broad shouldered and tough. From age thirteen to twenty, I tried different ones on, never leaving until a new prospect came along who might love me better than the last. I met Eric after my high school graduation, sprawled out on a blanket in the Metroparks. I was reading *The Four Loves* by C.S. Lewis—ever chasing after love—and there he was with those blue eyes and electricity and dust. He bought me jewelry and clothes, bicycles and fancy meals and plane tickets, converting his paychecks into love. I sopped it up like a too-long-dry mop. He drank. He smoked. He hid cans of chew. He touched me like I was precious and carried me up to his room. My dad thought he was the greatest. I did too—he planted me on the coast of Lake Erie and held me, listened to me, watched me, adored me. I watched the sunset with him. I read him my poetry and he drew pictures of islands and sunsets. He took me places I had never been, and we dreamed of going far away, traveling the world together, the two of us always together forever.

But he only tolerated my growing faith in a Christian God, on his own crusade to find Margaritaville, flying from Hawaii to Australia to New Zealand to Vietnam to Thailand and home and then off again. I had never lived outside of Ohio and attended school at a small Midwestern university, majoring in creative writing, reading every book assigned in literature classes. I worshipped God on Sunday mornings and Eric the rest of the weekend. *It's okay*, I thought, I loved him enough to make up for the rest. He worked harder and harder to lose me, and I kept hanging on, expecting something to change. And then it did. And then we were through.

I cried and cried, and Dad said, "I don't understand why you couldn't be with Eric."

6.

"Sare!" the voice mail began, a yell over the commotion of a crowd, "We're at Buck Owens' Crystal Palace."

Dad shouted across the wavelengths between Bakersfield, California, and Akron, Ohio, "and this girl's singin' . . . " a buzz of audience, then, "Listen."

Underneath the din of bodies laughing and yelling I could hear a female voice, the beat of a bass drum, the twang of country western, but the words were lost. It lasted a minute or two. I imagined my father standing with my mom in that cavernous space we visited when I was sixteen, holding his flip phone up in the direction of the stage, tipping back an amber bottle while the singer carried her tune. The place was full of bodies now, dark and foggy and loud. A rustle as Dad turned the phone back to his bristled cheek, "Okay," he grunted, "See you later."

That's it? I replayed the message again, time sent, two in the morning. I leaned in closer to my phone and covered my right ear to try to isolate the singer that prompted my father to dial my number in the midst of the concert. Just noise. Did he call because he remembered we had been there over a decade ago? Did he call because she was singing a song I should know, a song that would *mean* something to me, to us? Was it a message I should save? I played it again.

"Listen to this message from my dad," I said to my husband. "Listen to it. Can you hear what she's singing?" I replayed the message, this time on speakerphone. "Can you hear it?"

"Sare," Dad said each time, "Listen."

Building Fires

"I will bring that group through the fire and make them pure.
I will refine them like silver and purify them like gold."

— ZECH 13:9A NLT

WE'RE SIPPING WHISKEY ON our back patio, my husband of ten years and me, the summer light dwindling. The fire I tried to build in our pit is mostly smoke and the occasional flicker of flame licking at kindling. I keep poking it, repositioning logs, and twisting sheets of newspaper, but the log that was left in the outdoor fire pit spent all night (and the previous nine months) in the elements as June thunderstorms rolled through Northeast Ohio. The logs stacked around it won't ignite either.

It has been a strange season for us, a season of uncertainty, a season of new opportunities, a season of change. I send text messages to a friend while my husband picks the guitar and sings. His songs are carried away on the breeze. I readjust the logs into a sturdier pyramid.

A fire's intensity and the color of its flames depend on the substances burning and the quality of the environment. Paper and wood burn hottest near the surface—a bright white—then cool through the color spectrum from yellow to gold to orange and red. The blue flame produced by gasses like butane and propane burn even hotter.

You can light almost anything on fire if you douse it in lighter fluid. I'm not usually a butane gal; I want the hard-earned pleasure of a fire I built with matches, kindling, and logs. It isn't rubbing sticks together, but still, it's a challenge and an art to build a fire that will last for hours. My husband keeps playing his guitar. I catch lyrics here and there about love, burning

17

ring of fire love. The dry wood I've pulled from the log pile is hardly blackening. I keep poking it, crumpling paper, jamming kindling in underneath, and blowing on the embers, to see if I can't get a spark to light the wood on fire.

Back in college after my breakup with Eric, I had told myself that I would only date good Christian boys, guys that held in their hearts some kind of faith-based understanding of God so that we were at least able to communicate in the same language. Every serious conversation with Eric had been difficult, like shouting at each other from opposite sides of a chasm, me on the Mount of Olives, Eric on the peak of Margaritaville.

But Brandon held my hand as we worshipped in church. I grinned and listened to his strong voice belt out praise songs, squeezed his fingers entwined with mine. Brandon knew Scripture, attended church, graduated from a Christian high school, and had an intense passion for justice. He seemed like the kind of person I could lean into and he'd hold firm. This level of intimacy and depth had been missing from my former dating relationships. Praying out loud holding his hands with my eyes shut felt a bit like slicing open my chest and bearing the beating of my heart to him.

And to God, of course.

God would be front and center in this relationship, we told each other. We'd done it wrong before, put others in front of God, but no more. He was the third member of our conversations, as if God just stood up from the dining room table and we were talking about him while he was going to the bathroom. What did God want us to do? Let's make sure we are seeking God's will in this. If it doesn't seem like God's will for us to get married, we'll break up.

Also, all I wanted to do was make out with him. Brandon, that is. There was that, too, that added tension, that thrill of being pressed up against the door of his black Ford Mustang in the parking lot of the cinema, kissing and hugging and groping. From the passenger seat I cranked the radio, blasted the air-conditioning, and watched him shift and accelerate with one hand on the steering wheel and another on the stick. I rested my hand on his hand and flitted my fingers over his neck, up and down his leg.

After ten days with Brandon I was certain he was the man I would marry. We danced late into the night at the Boot Scoot'n Saloon, then watched a movie together on the futon in his parents' basement. The movie turned from upright to sideways as we kissed, our bodies wedged into the crevice of the couch. I paused for a second, breathless.

"How many people have you slept with?" I whispered. I was afraid he would say no one, afraid when he found out I'd slept with other men he would condemn me, even though I knew he had been engaged before. That might not mean anything, I thought, because Christians weren't supposed to have sex before they were married. This is what I had heard from the Christian subculture I entered when I went off to college—sex was my most precious gift to my future husband, and I had already thrown my virginity away. What if he hadn't had sex yet? Friends of mine had saved themselves for marriage; others hadn't and dated guys that rejected them when they found out, *damaged goods*, they said, *second hand*. I wanted our relationship to remain pure . . . but.

My high school boyfriend and I tried everything we could that wasn't *actually* sex. Then it was just a few seconds in the dark, then panic as we pulled away from one another, then emptiness. I was supposed to convert to Christianity; we were supposed to get married; we were supposed to wait. We didn't. After we broke up and I met Eric, sex was the hook that stuck the longest, the bond of that intimacy the hardest from which to yank free. I had already given myself away so fully; how could I get any of me back?

Brandon hesitated, then said, "Four. You?"

I sighed with relief. "Two," and we kept on kissing. My hands explored his curves, the nape of his neck, the line down his spine. Brandon had failed, too, failed at resisting the desire to be intimate with the person he had asked to marry him before he met me, the person he loved with his soul and mind and spirit and body, all connected and therefore painfully broken when it ended. The same way it left me, with Eric, shattered.

It seemed like we had known each other much longer than ten days. We had talked for hours about our futures, our dreams, and our hopes; we met each other's families and spent time with each other's friends. I already adored him, quick to awaken love, quick to hand over my heart.

"I love you," I whispered.

"I love you, too," he said. I wanted him. He wanted me. He retrieved a condom from his nightstand.

Breathless afterward, I thought how we seemed made for each other. My heart rate gradually slowed, and as the adrenaline decreased, guilt encroached. *What was I thinking? What did we do?* I retrieved my clothes and slipped back under the blankets, afraid to be seen. We tucked in close to each other under his down comforter until dawn.

The desire to become as intimate as possible with God was equally as strong as our desire to be as intimate as possible with each other. These two desires ran parallel in intensity but in constant tension, like two magnetic strips whose same poles are facing. "Let's Get It On" by Marvin Gaye and "Shout to the Lord" by Hillsong Australia played on the same mix CD Brandon made for me for my birthday. We were crazy for each other but kept up pretenses; after making out on the couch in his parents' basement, I crept back upstairs to the guest bedroom to sleep.

After getting it on the night before, we shouted to the Lord in the morning. We passed the communion wine and wafers. I raised a silent, desperate prayer for forgiveness, self-control, *Lord, lead us not into temptation but deliver us from evil*. We talked about being better disciplined, shook our heads at each other and smiled. Later on as the sports announcers called the baseball game, the blankets would hide us; it would be dark and quiet in the basement.

The rest of the time, we went to movies and Indians games, golfed, line danced, ate dinner out, and played Scrabble. He was my new hope for the future. If we were chemical bonds, then we were more covalent than ionic, as if we were sharing ourselves instead of exchanging parts of ourselves in order to make the other person whole.

I could never get enough of him. In the afternoons when classes were through for the day, I sent text messages asking about his plans for the night, which athletic teams were playing at home or away, if he minded some company, even if it was over an hour drive. *I can be there, no problem, just give me a minute and I'll see you by half-time.*

Nothing is more frustrating than trying to light a fire with green wood. Hardwoods and softwoods vary in the amount of time it takes for them to cure. I suspect the wood piled up on our patio is hardwood. It's been a year since it was cut, maybe less, and hardwoods take at least that long if not two years to dry out enough to burn clean. Freshly cut wood is about 50 percent water and won't burn; it leaves everyone dancing around the fire pit every time the wind shifts trying to avoid the plumes of smoke. The drier the wood, the cleaner the burn.

It's hard to rush the drying process. You can put one-inch thick green timber into a wood-drying kiln and get it down to a moisture content of 18 percent in ten hours. But hardwoods like oaks, solid masses of wood that burn long and slow, the kind of wood that once ignited will burn well into the night, it could take as long as twenty-eight days to dry down. You have to be patient.

Early on, Brandon and I dragged out the baggage of our pasts and unpacked "two" and "four" so we could survey the contents and then close up the suitcases. We talked about our exes in footnotes and afterthoughts; they appeared in rear-view mirrors and haunted radio stations. I knew enough about his ex to be trained to hate her for the way she'd treated him. He proposed to Devin twice and she ended it twice. *She was always changing her hair color*, he spat. They listened to Dave Matthews sing "Crash Into Me." She kept the ring he gave her, *Probably pawned it by now*, he said, shaking his head. Brandon took a job in Texas to try to make a break and start over. He had just moved back to Ohio about a month before we met. He said his ex was crazy. I said mine didn't care about God, not about my version of God, anyway.

When Jimmy Buffett or Dave Matthews came on the radio, we changed the station.

I still thought about Eric. I wondered what he was doing and whether he was traveling somewhere, whether my prayers after dreams about him had reached into his spirit and wedged open a crack so the light might get in. It had been seven months since we broke up. The burn in my chest over that loss had subsided to a cooling ember, but if I blew on it a bit, the flame was still there.

Brandon and I had been dating three months when he decided to trade in his Mustang. Winter was coming. We strolled the car lot and took a couple of test drives. The salesman invited the loan officer over to explain the way the loan would work, how the trade-in would result in negative equity, but no problem, driving a rear-wheel-drive Mustang in Northeast Ohio winters is dangerous. He *needed* this truck. Brandon would get a lower interest rate if I cosigned on the loan.

We looked into each other's eyes and asked, "Are we in this together for the long haul?" and then grinned and signed the papers. We drove off with our fingers interlaced in our brand-new, dark-red Ford Ranger. It was four-wheel drive, tough enough for the Snowbelt and his forty-five-minute commute from Akron to his job at a Christian high school near Solon. I inhaled the new-car smell and our future together, engaged by Christmas, married by the same time next year.

Three days later, Brandon wanted to break up.

I was in my last year of my undergraduate career. Brandon worked as an athletic director about sixty miles away. When he was at his desk we instant messaged each other on AOL. He was quiet most of the day online before I asked him if I could come up to watch the soccer game that night. His message back and then his phone call said, "I need a break. I need some space to sort things out."

I didn't know what to say. "Why? What happened?"

He gave no reason. That was it. A break. Separating. Space. The kindling cooled and went out, burnt flecks of paper lifting in the wind.

I hung up, tucked the phone in close beside me in my bed, and sobbed. *What just happened? We need a break?! We just co-signed on a loan! Three days ago! We were talking about getting married and having babies! What happened between then and now to cause this sudden breakdown?* I had given myself over to another person, who no longer wanted me. I crawled under my blankets and wept into my pillow.

I didn't want to eat dinner and instead dove into a Christian novel, disappearing into the first-century tale of a Jewish Christian girl in love with the arrogant son of the Roman couple to which she was enslaved. She was the picture of faith in isolation, unconditional love, patience, self-control. She had mastered purity.

I thought about Eric. Maybe these seven months were just enough for him to have his own come-to-Jesus moment, maybe he realized now what a perfect pair we'd be, worshipping and praying together, going to church, reading the Bible and discussing the ways in which God had been so good to us, looking back and seeing his hand heavy on our lives, how he had been shoring up our foundations and laying down a boardwalk toward a future with us together. I had a taste of that kind of a relationship, even though it was unraveling in front of me. Maybe this relationship with Brandon, both of us damaged but still connected to our exes, was simply an opportunity to heal together and then part ways better people. A lot can happen in seven months, I reasoned. Maybe *this,* not this other thing, was God's will. I blew my nose and wiped my eyes, put my hand on my cell phone, lifted it and dropped it on the bed, picked it up again.

❀

During one of the times Eric and I were "just friends" (*with benefits,* he winked) his mom had told me about their pre-marriage days. His dad and mom had spent a year apart and didn't talk to test out their commitment to one another. Was it love? Was it hard enough, strong enough, thick enough to weather a year of silence and then burn forever? I wanted a marriage like theirs. I wanted Eric to have faith in God, to be the man I knew he could be. She understood.

After a Thursday night worship service, I dialed Eric's mother's number as I paced in front of the dorm. I was anxious to hear about him—months had passed since I'd spoken to him or his family—but made small talk about school instead. It was chilly outside and dark, other college students coming and going from the dorm building as I paced, my arms crossed against my chest, shivering. Finally I asked, "How's Eric?"

"He just got a job this fall on a golf course and moved to North Carolina," she said.

I sighed, ashamed. "That's great! That's just what he wanted to do. I'm so happy for him."

Perched on the picnic table outside with the phone closed in my hand, I cried again. How could I cry upstairs in my bed—sobbing, jolted tears—over Brandon, whom I had confessed to love enough to marry someday, and think in the same exhale that maybe this was my chance to get back together with Eric? Was my "love" that shallow? Was its flame so fickle?

I flicked through the Bible that had traveled with me since the fall of my freshman year. So many verses, so many promises. I had underlined line after line. A verse written on a fragment of paper from a worship service in Australia slipped out, a bookmark on the page in Malachi where I'd underlined, "'Bring the whole tithe into the storehouse, that there may be food in my house. Test me in this,' says the Lord Almighty, 'and see if I will not throw open the floodgates of heaven and pour out so much blessing that there will not be room enough to store it.'"

Maybe it was a sign. How could I render this Scripture verse to address the hurt I felt? I thought about the times I felt like I had compromised my faith, how many times Brandon and I had slept together even though we felt guilty for doing so, even though I had promised myself I'd wait, again, until it was made right by marriage. Had I *really* tried to stay pure? Had I brought everything to God these last few months? *Okay, Lord,* I sighed, *I will hand this over. Open the floodgates.*

I spent the weekend after Brandon and I broke up in Pittsburgh with a friend I met in Australia. She knew me when I was chasing Eric; she knew me as I struggled to discern God's will for my relationships and for my life, scribbling in my prayer journal like shaking a Magic 8-Ball for answers. She had also met Brandon. It felt good to escape for a while, to watch movies on her couch in her apartment and talk through the details of the last week.

There was the problem of the cosigned truck. There was the call to Eric's mom. There was my love for Brandon and our combined desire for God's will in our relationship.

It was true that I still loved Eric. If he had been in Ohio and interested in seeing me, I might have even gone to him, just to see if things had changed. But those embers simmered. That fire was dying. This one with Brandon was new but so full of potential.

By the end of the weekend, I felt a sense of peace. Whatever happened, I would be okay. I would be *okay*. Really? Really. Okay. If it meant alone or if it meant with him, I'd resurface. I'd survive. I'd love again. This was new, this strength and resolve, this sense of identity and resilience separate from a man.

My dad called me while I drove out of Pittsburgh, a city I had never navigated on my own.

"You cosigned on a loan with this guy and now he's *gone?* You broke up?!" he yelled.

"I thought we were going to get married! I thought this meant that an engagement ring would be coming soon!" I tried to explain through tears, screaming back into the phone. "What do you want me to say?"

"You have to get out of that loan, Sarah," Dad said, and I turned blindly onto the highway, accelerating through the onramp and construction zones. Dad still wasn't sure about this city guy who showed up in his fast car, pressed pants and dress shirt, expensive sunglasses. Dad still wondered why it didn't work out with Eric. But Brandon had a truck, right? and he listened to country music; he could talk sports and politics with the best of them, and sure, he'd take a beer. He was *usually* solid, *usually* steadfast, firm and trustworthy, like Dad. He was tough, smart, stubborn, funny, passionate, faithful. This is what Dad had modeled for me. He was also distant, busy, hard-working, slow to demonstrate his affections. This, too.

"I'll figure something out," I said, wiping my eyes. "Just give me some time." I looked around and realized somehow I had gotten on the highway, headed in the right direction, back toward Ohio. I didn't know what to do about the loan, but I knew one thing: I would not chase this relationship down into the ground, like every other boyfriend before Brandon. He could run to me, if he wanted.

❊

And then I called him. We needed to figure out something about the truck. It was a good excuse.

"Can I come by? I have some of your stuff and you have some of mine."

We hovered near the doorway as I prepared to leave. He was wearing fleece pants and a t-shirt; he slouched and hung his head. He didn't say a lot but looked at me with the saddest eyes. I didn't want to act cool and unemotional.

"I don't understand what's going on," I said quietly, "but I want to give you the space you need to sort it out." I believed myself when I said this.

"Why do you love me?" he asked, staring deep into my eyes. No man had ever looked so forlorn. It was astounding to me, to see him so sad and yet *he* was the one who had put our relationship on pause. I thought for a long time. What could I say? Nothing he did for me, not the way he made me feel, nothing he gave me or called me came to mind as enough of a reason for loving him the way I did, for feeling so sure about who we were together. Our backgrounds were completely different: I was raised in the country. He was raised in the city. He was an athlete. I was a book nerd. But we loved music. We loved to dance. We made each other laugh. He was a worthy Scrabble opponent. We wanted the same things in life—a spouse, a family, stability. To each of our desires we said, *Me too.* Our many differences seemed to complement rather than to rub up against each other. It even felt like God's will to me that we should be together.

And oh, how he made me *feel*. I could see us looking in the same direction into the future; I could see us giving each other the room to be the people we were capable of being. And that's what I loved: Possibility. Potential. Hope. Maybe I could find that with someone else, too. But I didn't want to.

I shrugged my shoulders and looked in those sad eyes, "I really don't know, but I do love you, I don't know why I love you, but I do," and I gathered my things and headed out the front door.

In the weeks we were apart, I wrote a letter to Brandon about our previous loves, about packs of matches stricken on flint, about the quick spark and burn and ash. And I wrote to him about the love I hoped to have with him. There was no fast flame, no stream of lighter fluid sprayed and ignited— we met at a church picnic, after all—it was a relationship that could grow the way you build a bonfire, layers of kindling and thinner limbs, a big, well-seasoned, all-nighter log placed on top only after you have it good and stoked and then that log will stay hot for hours after you thought it should've died. The mornings after such a fire, you can poke the coals in the middle and they'll still glow, still reignite with a little more timber. *I will wait for you. I believe in us. We could have this kind of love.*

Three weeks after we split up, we went out—as friends—with a group of people to line dance at the Boot. *Okay*, I thought, *I can do this.* I went to our friends' house beforehand to get ready.

"I don't know what his problem is," Jen said, "He's crazy."

We stared at our reflections in the mirror, applying mascara and lipstick, surveying our profiles. I wasn't sure what I expected from the night out, but I knew Brandon would be there. I dressed in tight blue jeans and a halter top, just in case. Maybe we could be friends.

The guys began stacking beer bottles along the bar. I spun back and forth on a stool with my black underage Sharpie X's on my hands, conscious of the five-year age gap between me and his friends. When "Steam" by Ty Herndon came on, I sprang from my stool and grapevined alone, stomping my feet and gyrating my hips with sideways glances to see if Brandon was watching.

Then the DJ played a waltz. Brandon grabbed my hand and pulled me close. We danced around the floor, our faces away from each other until he turned my jaw in for a kiss. I wanted to melt into it, but we were supposed to be "taking a break." Was the break over? I left the floor before the song ended to try to compose myself in the bathroom.

By the time I returned to the dance floor, the lights had dimmed, and Brandon took my hand again. His strong voice bellowed into my ear as he sang along and we swayed. Whatever had happened didn't matter; this was where I wanted to be, safe and warm in his arms.

"Where have I been?" he said, his breath close on my neck.

It was so loud in the bar and my voice hardly carries, so I yelled, "Is this where you belong?"

He hugged me tight and kissed me again, "I love you."

"Promise?"

We held hands in the car on the way back to his place, just like before. We made love, then slipped into separate beds, just like before. We held hands in church the next morning and all the way back home, just like before. I wanted to leave it be, to forget that a month had passed since we broke up on the phone, to just fold into him and go forward as if nothing happened. He caressed my forehead while we watched a movie in the basement until I fell asleep on the couch. When I woke, I nuzzled his neck and smiled.

"What more could a guy want?" he said.

I turned to look into his eyes. "What happened the last month?" I asked. "I am loving this, and I'm so glad we're back together, but what happened, babe?"

Brandon's ex-fiancée had called him the afternoon we broke up. "I went to her house, and at first it was great again but then I realized nothing had changed. She was exactly the same; we were exactly the same."

I saw myself standing on the sidewalk outside of my dorm on the phone, hoping, *maybe something had changed.* My heart ached. "I know, I know what you went through," I confessed, crying, telling him about the phone call. "If Eric had called me, I would have done the same thing."

We held each other for a long time.

"If we are going to try to make this work, I think we should stop sleeping together, stop making out," Brandon said. I nodded. I had said the same words to Eric months into our relationship—no more sex—and failed again and again. This time would be different; on Brandon's lead, we would date according to what we felt was God's will—to purify what we'd made impure—and see what surfaced. He wanted to know if he loved me or just lusted for me, to know each other more than in bed, to feed a different kind of fire between us.

"Come on, just kiss me!" I teased, standing in the doorway to the basement stairwell. Brandon squeezed my waist and clenched his teeth.

"Be gone, evil temptress!" he said with a grin.

That was what I wanted, wasn't it? Purity. To know that what we built between us was greater than lust, stronger than a longing passion to satisfy each other's physical desires. *Stay pure!* The self-help guides for Christian dating shouted. *Kiss dating goodbye!* But when you have been longing for so *long* to be loved wholly—as far back as thirteen, when that first boy kissed your lips in the movie then plunged his tongue in between, then slipped his thick hands up your shirt and then reached for your pants button but then the movie ended, and you left frozen—when someone comes along who loves you wholly, finally, oh, how the heart and body yearn to be touched.

We stopped touching. We fought the urges to love each other physically for nine months, almost until our wedding day. Almost.

Inside I burned, *love me love me love me*, leaning in for a kiss at the top of his steps, "Be gone, evil temptress!" Brandon said between his teeth, desire set in that jaw line I loved, and I left, dejected and hungry, to sleep in the spare bedroom.

"I don't understand why you can't even *kiss* me," I pouted.

"It's like a switch for me," he said, "I'm either on or off." And *off* was the setting of necessity, until we settled on whether it was indeed God's will for us to spend the rest of our lives together.

Weeks before our wedding day, we gave in again to each other, bodies hot and tired of resisting for so long. Afterward, the wall of guilt and shame resurrected again. We failed. *Dear God, forgive us*, we prayed, *forgive us our sins, lead us not into temptation. Purify us.*

The purifying process is complex. Rarely is gold or silver found in its purest form in nature. The process of extracting gold from large chunks of rock involves pulverizing the rock into powder, mixing the powder with chemicals, rinsing and sifting the gold with more chemicals and water, and finally melting the gold in a furnace at around 2,100 degrees Fahrenheit in a process called smelting. This results in a bar of near-pure gold. In order to process gold into its purest form, these bars are sent to refineries, where they are melted again in a furnace, mixed with borax and soda ash in order to separate out the pure gold from any remaining minerals or semi-precious metals, and then tested to ensure the gold is now 99.9 percent pure.

Can you imagine that degree of heat, the intensity of *that* flame? If the spirit is to be refined by God into pure gold, then the vices that cling to the human spirit are broad and diverse, semi-precious and common, easily mistaken like fool's gold for the real thing. The refining process burns away all vices and purifies the spirit of unrighteousness. This process is slow, exhaustive, tedious. Life-long.

From this distance, I know that this degree of self-control was necessary for the two of us. We were so quick to give over ourselves to others, so quick to seek out intimacy. Abstinence together for this purpose—to test the worth of our love—laid the foundation for our marriage. But the burn of guilt and shame when we failed was tarnish on metal, it was residual rock, it was waste.

What I know now is that purity is not just abstinence. Purity is not something held once and then lost, damaged, secondhand. The power of the Cross is not that we might strive for perfection and receive our reward based on how good we've been. The power of the Cross is that we are free from the burden of perfection and made holy and pure through the redemptive love, grace, and mercy of Christ. Not because of anything we've done, not because we've resisted temptation, not because we waited until marriage, but only because of Christ. Only because of the Father's love. Only because of the power of the Holy Spirit.

I can't regret for myself anymore the decisions I made to have sex before I married Brandon. Maybe I regret how *long* I spent seeking after a person who no longer loved me back, how *deep* my need for his affection was rooted. But that particular crisis drove me to my knees, it released me from the grip of "do good things" and delivered me into the garden of *I have loved you with an everlasting love; I have drawn you with unfailing kindness.* Not condemnation. How can I live in regret when it was out of that dirt that God delivered me into his garden?

I am a body and a soul and a mind and a spirit, and I am meant to love with all of me, love my God and my neighbor and myself. And my husband.

The water soaked log still isn't burning, but at least it's propping up the other logs, now aflame in their pyramid shape, no longer relying on quick bursts of heat from paper or smaller sticks. The light evening breeze catches the embers and ignites them into golden tongues licking the wrought iron fire pit. It is mostly flame with a little smoke, which occasionally drifts our direction. We turn our faces away to keep the fumes from tearing up our eyes. My clothes and hair will smell like this fire when I climb into bed tonight beside Brandon, and neither of us will care. We just spent a few hours in the crisp night air by a blazing source of heat, singing and playing music and drinking whiskey, our children asleep inside, my phone closed now to the outside world. We are being smelted, after all. A little water-logged wood can't keep us down.

When the wind shifts again, I watch the smoke curl off of the damp log, the embers glowing red and white and black and red again when the wind sweeps over them. I listen to the soothing crackle as sparks lift into the air. From here the flames are just a touch of warmth carried with a chill, but the logs are on fire now and set to burn as long as we stoke them, gold flames kissing the darkening sky.

Bobby Pins

FOR THE FIRST TIME we were alone. Hair stylists and photographers, brides-maids and groomsmen, the caterer and DJ, parents, family, and friends followed us throughout the morning, all afternoon, and late into the evening. We exchanged rings and vows, lit a candle and took communion, posed for more photos, rode in a limo, ate and danced and cut cake and danced and danced and danced until finally, we climbed into our red Ford Ranger, coated in butter by our prankster groomsmen, and drove away, husband and wife, bride and groom, alone.

The concierge at Walden Inn in Aurora led us back to the villa Brandon's parents had reserved for us. We admired the space we'd enjoy together for the next twelve hours before heading back to my parents' house to open gifts, wall-length windows overlooking thick woods, a loft where we'd sleep, sofa and fireplace down below, Jacuzzi tub and double shower, soft, warm light. Champagne and chocolate covered strawberries waited on the table. There were rose petals everywhere, on the floor, on the bed, around the Jacuzzi tub.

We each took a glass and a strawberry and turned away from each other as we undressed. I unlatched all that had held me tight throughout the day, unzipped and unsnapped and let fall away, then turned shy toward my groom, my husband.

Shy, even though this was long before the days of stretch marks and cellulite blossoming down my sides, weight gained and lost, surgeries and caesareans and scars. These were the days of no makeup and unmaintained hair, running because it was fun, eating whatever I wanted. Our bodies were lean, our skin smooth and taut against muscle and bone. Shy, even after our early acquaintance under blankets in his parents' basement, tangling naked between sheets and then slipping off quickly to redress before being seen. Upon undressing with the man I had been most intimate with,

31

every perceived imperfection rose to the surface, every unfair comparison with other women bubbled into consciousness: maybe my thighs are too wide, maybe my breasts are too small, maybe my butt is too big, maybe I'm too jello-y around the middle.

These are our bodies. I want to shake that girl standing beside the bathtub naked, ready to immerse herself in the bubbling water as fast as possible so she can be covered. Her wedding dress is a cloud of satin, taffeta, and tulle on the floor, her strapless bra and simple lace underwear fall to her feet. There she stands, naked, exposed, for the first time in front of her groom, and she is shy, self-conscious, insecure.

You are beautiful, I want to say, *don't you know that you are a miraculous machine of neurons and synapses and blood vessels and muscles and skin, marrow and bone, unique and imperfect and lovely in your youth and in your aging, too, you are a body and a mind and a spirit and a soul, and each part is precious, valuable, worthy, and this is your husband who has chosen you, all of you, loves all of you, each and every part of you.*

But even the woman who wants to utter these words today shies away from the mirror, slips underneath the blankets, hidden.

The water was hot and made my skin glow pink. Brandon slid in behind me. I leaned my head against his chest.

"Could you help me take out the bobby pins in my hair?" I asked. One by one, Brandon picked out a hundred brown and black clips that had kept each curl and ringlet in place throughout the day. The soap bubbles around us fizzled and popped. Slowly each strand fell down.

I could have stood over the sink and picked each pin from my up-do myself, arms raised above my head, fingertips exploring my scalp for the clips, but instead, I rested my head against my husband's chest and he slowly undid all that had been done, pin by pin.

This is who he is with me; he might be loud and opinionated and aggressive and competitive in front of other men and women, but here, he is gentle, careful, loosens the layers of stiffness and protection I've applied and gathers what remains of me—exposed, exhausted, vulnerable, and soft—into himself.

My hair felt crispy and the roots ached from holding their place for so long. When he was done, I shook loose the mass of hairspray and gel and dipped underneath the surface to remove some of the stickiness, wash away the layer of makeup. Rising above again, mascara melted down my cheeks. All that was left of what had hidden me washed down the drain. We lifted ourselves out of the tub and climbed the stairs to the bedroom loft, our bodies warm between the sheets.

Uprooted

MOM AND I WALK around our house in Ashland one summer Sunday surveying the landscape. When Brandon and I moved in several years ago, overgrown burning bushes and box-shaped yews dominated the front flower beds. We sawed them down to ground level, then planted around the stumps—rhododendrons, hydrangea, and river birch the most prominent plants, Knock-Out roses, Stella d'Oro daylilies, and hostas I split and divided over the course of a couple years bordering the beds. Recently, I noticed a powdery white substance collecting on the river birch's leaves.

We planted a similar tree at my parents' house ten years ago, but now, Mom said, it was causing problems. The river birch dropped its seed pods all over the deck in the spring; in the summer, its little green flowers fell. Then Japanese beetles came and ate all of its leaves, their droppings littered all over the patio furniture. *It's disgusting,* Mom said. Dad wanted to cut it down or dig it out with the backhoe.

I chose the river birch. Its bark peels away in cinnamon colored strips, like shedding skin, leaving behind a previous identity and embracing a new one. The leaves are glossy green with serrated edges that cast shadows interrupted with beams of light. Its multiple trunks share the same root system. The river birch is my favorite. It's a medium- to fast-growing tree, and big, maybe too big for the spot we planted it at my parents. Like my own home's landscaping, it was the center point of the bed; we planned the remaining layout around the tree.

When I came home from college that spring ten years ago, I brought back the baggage of my ended relationship with Eric. Mom and I pushed our spade shovels into the earth and turned the soil over together. We wiped the sweat from our foreheads and drank water in gulps. We moved two rhododendrons into the shade of the river birch, split hostas and daylilies and arranged them, dug a path and laid a walkway to the deck. We left the climbing hydrangea that Eric had given her even though it never produced any flowers and still hadn't, even in the decade it'd been there. Maybe it wasn't planted in the right type of soil.

If Dad cut down the river birch, perhaps a flowering crab apple would do better, or another ornamental, like the Japanese maple we planted to remember my grandfather. But the Japanese maple lasted one season and then froze up, one lousy green sucker at the base of the trunk while the rest of the canopy stood naked. Maybe a dogwood instead, although those are susceptible to disease, too, and the good ones aren't cheap. The fact is I can't imagine that landscape without the river birch.

As late afternoon approached, Mom and Dad got in their car to make the hour and a half trip back to Auburn Township, back home along the seventy-mile stretch of highway. I would have liked to invite them to stay for dinner, too, stay until the sun crept west and landed with a splash in the star-studded June sky, stay for drinks after the kids went to bed, stay to stand around a fire pit and tell stories until the air is filled with long pauses and loud yawns. But we live in Ashland, and they live in Auburn. The towns are closer in the dictionary than they are geographically.

My two brothers live within a mile of my parents' house and the family farm in Auburn. Given my brothers' proximity to my parents, coming over for dinner, stopping by for a drink, or hanging out in the garage is quick, easy, and casual. To arrange the same visit with us calls for planning around the kids' nap schedules and packing bags to stay the night in order to avoid driving three hours in one day.

I am envious of their closeness. I want to "just drop by" because I "happened to be in the neighborhood." I'd like to be able to call fifteen minutes before I leave the house to make sure they're home, to stop on my way from work to talk about the day or grill a few burgers together. But like most people in their late twenties and thirties, we moved away from our families after we got married in pursuit of jobs that would sustain us. We started our own family in a town without grandmas and sought out good and cheap daycares and babysitters. We chose to leave what is familiar for the unknown, to strike out beyond the present in order to make a future.

I take my daughter, Lydia, out on my brother's four-wheeler through my grandmother's field across the street from my parents' home. It's another summer evening, the long kind. We throttle down the lanes and over the bumpy harvested cornfields, the severed stalks jutting up before Dad or Uncle Frank has had a chance to plow them under. She giggles as we accelerate down the hill toward my aunt's house and turn to ride along the perimeter of the woods. I slow to a stop and let the engine idle a minute, watching the fallow field for deer. The sun is beginning to set over the hill, so we start back up toward my parents' house. We pass the rusting, abandoned trailer just inside the woods and circle back around a stretch of brush separating the top of the hill from the bottom. A groundhog scurries back into its hole near the pile of boulders overgrown with tufts of grass and wildflowers.

Driving back up the hill along the tree line, the warm summer air blowing our hair back, Lydia tucked in close between me and the steering wheel, it all takes me back to riding with my dad on another four-wheeler, bumping along the packed earth roads between crops, sometimes sandwiched in front of him and other times hanging on tight to the sides of his shirt or gripping the handlebars on the back. I raced my brother on snowmobiles through that same field, adrenaline rushing, snow dusting up behind us, cold air and snowmobile exhaust filling my lungs through the scarf over my face.

As a young girl, my grandmother straddled her father's giant workhorse and rode him from her home on the corner of their sixty-four-acre farm to her grandma's house on top of the hill. The weight of his plodding hoofs would have left a trail of horseshoe prints up the hill in the impressionable spring dirt. It is the same hill we climb on the four-wheeler, leaving behind our own set of tracks in the mud that will be erased in the next hard rain, the same earth farmed by our family for the last 150 years.

Over the rumble of the four-wheeler, Lydia and I hear dozens of Canada geese cawing and honking at each other in the wheat. As we reach the crest of the hill, we slow a little and listen, watch the golden light slivering through the trees, the geese squawking, and then we rev the four-wheeler again, the geese lighting into the summer evening, angry about being disturbed. The geese stop in this field during migration every year; it's as if they make a point of visiting on their way south, honk and call to one another from either end of the V every evening, *this is the place, stop here, it is beautiful, remember?* They also leave each year, depart for somewhere north, somewhere south, somewhere else.

We cross the ditch and the paved street and ride through my parents' yard to park the four-wheeler, our legs and arms still vibrating from the engine, my heart still beating from the thrill of the land, the geese, the feel of my daughter's head under my chin. Soon we need to scavenge the house for dirty clothes and discarded toys, pack our bags, and leave the place I still call home in order to drive south to the place my daughter calls home.

❋

Surrounding my parents' house are the houses of my ancestors. Over 150 years ago, one set of my ancestors left Charleston, New York, the place they called home, and journeyed to the Western Reserve, to the newly settled Geauga County in Northeast Ohio. Back then the trees that stretch high above me were probably saplings, maybe as thick as a young girl's wrists. The land on which they settled has been in our family since the mid-1800s. My grandmother has lived in the same blue farmhouse since she was three years old. Now, my dad and mom own the house across the street.

My great-great-great grandparents, Oliver and Catherine Davis, made their journey west to Ohio in the mid-1800s on a sleigh in February with nothing but a wood stove. They already had five children and Catherine was pregnant with another, their oldest child staying back in New York. Maybe the promise of a new start, a new adventure, or greater land opportunities prompted Oliver and Catherine to uproot their growing family. Whatever drove them west firmly rooted my extended family in the geography of Northeastern Ohio.

Until I moved away a decade ago, first to Akron and then to Ashland, stretching our roots seventy miles down Route 71. I am the farthest grandchild away from the family farm. When I come home to visit, I tend to drift from room to room in my parents' house. I look a little lost. I wander from picture frame to doorpost, every item a purpose, every object a memory, even the alterations a reminder of what used to be. The air carries a certain aroma I want to linger in. I want to be heady with it, overwhelmed by it. I never itch to leave or worry for something to do. I feel the heat escape from the metal grates, feel the pull of winter air against the plastic taped to the windows. This house and its surroundings hold our family history like DNA, every object's textures and folds embedded with memories. The weight of it sweeps and engulfs me, makes me want to stay tucked on my mother's couch underneath the crocheted blanket she made.

When I come to visit, my mom and the kids and I walk the length of the field where Grandma rode her horse between her house on the corner and her grandmother's home. The kids run through the yard where I used to play ghost in the graveyard, hide-and-go-seek, TV tag, and SPUD all summer. My cousins and I would scavenge through the three-season front porch to find the baseball mitts and wooden bats my aunts and uncles left behind. Now, my children rummage through the weeds to find a lost softball. My daughter plunks on the same upright piano where I practiced Do-Re-Mi and sang "The Camptown Ladies sing this song, Doo-Da, Doo-Da," inventing my own melody when I tired of "Oh, the doo-da day." The boys are giddy over the sand pile that's been stationed there underneath the maple tree for at least a half century. They climb and ride down a faded Little Tikes elephant slide that my now twenty-seven-year-old brother got for Christmas when he was two.

The landscape is thick with overgrown rhododendrons, heavily shaded by oaks and maples, grass fine and feathery where we barrel-rolled as kids, where my now husband and I stretched out and planned for the future a decade ago. The bleeding heart shrub still pushes out its blossoms every spring. The daffodils still bloom in the lawn along the limestone walk every May. Cousins and nieces and nephews still forage the yard and the fields and the woods, looking for and finding all kinds of trinkets, all kinds of treasure.

My husband and I didn't know how hard it would be to move from Akron, just ten minutes away from his parents and close enough to my family to make for an easy day visit, to a small town like Ashland, Ohio, and in November of all months, when families begin to hibernate in their homes. It had been four years since we were wed. In that time we'd acquired two dogs and re-homed one, lost two fetuses to miscarriage and welcomed two babies into our home. We'd bought a house and sold a house. We'd prepared for our first child, who threatened to be a premie but ended up coming late. Fifteen months later, we delivered our presumed healthy, full-term second child straight into the arms of the NICU nurses, and then spent two weeks waiting for him to breathe on his own. We'd weathered some things in our first four years of marriage. What's a little job change? What's a little move to a new city? What's a little role reversal?

The dozens of pieces that needed to fall in place for me to take the job as an administrative director at a university had landed perfectly—insurance secured, house sold, income increased—as if God himself had reached his hands down and cleared the way. Brandon quit his job and we packed up the portable storage unit. We expected to join a community ripe with social life, but it turned out that I was the only member of my department with young children, and everyone I interacted with on a day-to-day basis was off campus. There weren't departmental potlucks or afternoon mixers. It was cold, and we had an eighteen-month-old and a three-month-old. No one was outside, and no one wanted to be.

We forgot that moving meant a violent transplant of roots, a severing by the sudden jump and push of a round-point shovel into the earth, roots broken and shedding dirt in clumps, branches bending, leaves wilting and then shed.

We had no friends. We had no church connections. Brandon became the full-time, stay-at-home dad and held that role for nine months. He went from coaching high school sports every season of the year and teaching full-time to changing diapers, entertaining toddlers, mixing rice cereal, and maintaining nap schedules.

"I hate my life!" Brandon yelled, slamming the kitchen cabinet shut one morning as I prepared to go to work. Our daughter clanked her toddler spoon and fork against her high chair in the corner. Our son kicked his legs and punched the air with his fists in the bouncy seat on the table. I stared at him, standing there in his pajamas while I wore pressed pants and makeup.

I hustled out the door weeping but went to work anyway, retreating to the safe haven of my office where I did the work I felt called to do. For all of my life, I had expected to grow up and become Mrs. Anyone, to marry and be the stay-at-home parent, and that was it. But I loved my job. I didn't know that such a thing was possible, to love a job the way I loved my job. I loved my job, and I was good at it. In my office, I could escape the growing tension and depression in our little brick house and relish the satisfaction of feeling right where I belonged.

I knew things were harder at home than he anticipated. But mostly, I ignored it. I hoped he'd just get over it, or find work, *something*. Wasn't this what we bought into when we moved? What did he expect? And if this life was so bad, I thought angrily, why didn't he just leave and let us get on with our lives without his frustration, without his impatient bursts, door slamming, feet stomping? On nights I couldn't sleep and prostrated myself on the couch, crying into throw pillows, I whispered to God, *Let him go if he needs to. I could do this alone if I had to. I could make this work.*

When Oliver and Catherine Davis moved from New York in the middle of winter on a sleigh with their children, I imagine that their journey was filled with many unknowns. The Western Reserve was just beginning to be settled. They needed to clear land of the many trees to farm and build their home, needed to carefully select the land based on the location of creeks and the grade of the hills. Besides these preparations were the usual tasks of farm life. Farm families in the 1850s raised their own food, butchered their own meat, smoked their own ham and bacon, churned their own butter, made their own cheese, spun their own yarn, wove their own clothing, and made their own dye.

As the days and weeks and months wore on in Northeast Ohio, how did the large Davis family relate underneath the shelter of one roof? Were there long silences and brooding moods as the Northeastern Ohio winter settled in, burying the fields in heavy snow? Surely these people—my ancestors—sweat and swore, swept the floors, wooed and wed, bore babies in bedrooms, lost wives in labor and mourned. Did Oliver wander out to the barn for hours, muck out stalls, feed the horses and cattle while blowing hot air into the cup of his hands? Was Catherine watching for him through the falling snow outside her kitchen window, a hand draped across her swollen abdomen as she waited for yet another baby to arrive in the wilderness? No one records the long weeks and months that pass like one dark, foggy night, until finally, the sun creeps through the clouds, slowly burns off the dull ache that took residence for so long, and something close to resignation, or peace, or contentment, or possibly even joy returns.

What did Catherine miss about Charleston, New York? Did she miss her father back in New England? Did she miss the home and land of her childhood? Did she yearn to return to the shade trees, orchards, and fields of Charleston? Did she question their decision to uproot their family away from what had always been home? At night after her husband slept, did she sit awake underneath a quilt by the fire and doubt the wilderness and the opportunities it promised?

I don't think you can go on long in dark silence alone. Either the roots shrivel up, are split apart and repotted, or someone steps up and notices what is happening, waters you into the new landscape, braids new hope for your future. Winter begins to end. You find a church, some friends, a project or two to do. You drag the darkness into the light and make it face you.

※

The trick to leaving is knowing what to take with you and what to leave behind. Take bunches of split hostas and a lilac offshoot. Take a few pictures but leave room for new ones. Take the get up early to work in the garden but leave the silence between fights; leave, too, the power to remember every wrong. Take pride in the work but leave behind the sense that the hard work was never enough. Leave some photos and old stuffed animals, blankets, maybe even some old clothes in your closet, some bad poems and letters from friends at the bottom of a shoebox. Take your toothpaste, a travel deodorant, enough snacks for the car, and one extra change of clothes. Leave a few Matchbox cars and Tonka trucks in the sandbox for your son to find later on.

In a cemetery in South Newbury, what remains of my ancestors' bodies rests beneath dirt and sod, weathered tombstones, and shade trees. I learn this through my grandmother, who can recite her lineage from memory. She spins a tale from her childhood like it happened yesterday. She speaks as if I already know these people and have known them my whole life, like I met them when they were living even though they passed away decades before my birth. The more I research their lives and their times, the more I think I really *do* know them. I can feel the chill winter air swirling through the long ride in the woods, the warm breath of the horses puffing and steam rising off their bodies, see the stark whiteness of the wilderness under a new coat of snow. I am Catherine calming the children in the sleigh scolding when they start pinching each other out of boredom, braiding the girls' hair, shifting positions in the sled from left haunch to right, trying to keep comfortable in my pregnant body. I am Oliver leaving New York behind, hoping in things yet unseen. I am Catherine squeezing Oliver's calloused hand as he urges the horses on. I am Oliver staring into the trees, watching the snow drift and sway, the landscape changing, shifting, the world tilting, spinning quicker, my heart anxious for a home.

Brandon travels every week for work, now; we tag-team parent, handing off the kids and car keys each week, keeping in touch by text messages—*see you Sunday, love you too, pick up some bananas and eggs on your way home.* After he comes home and we renegotiate living together, relearn how to love and live in the same house, parent the same kids at the same time, load the dishwasher differently, fold the t-shirts in rectangles instead of squares, after all of this in the stillness and darkness and silence of night before he needs to leave again, I think maybe it would be easier to separate. I'm a single mom most of the time, anyway. He can have the kids on Monday, Tuesday, and Wednesday; I'll take them Thursday through Sunday. Make sure they get picked up from school. Here, watch them on Skype, here they are playing basketball. Say goodnight to Dad, kids, wherever he is, whichever city or time zone he's in. Easier because we wouldn't have to keep trying to make our lives together *work,* we wouldn't need to schedule in time to love each other, we wouldn't need to communicate through Google Calendar to make sure that our schedules don't overlap, and if they do, radio in to air traffic control because the landing strip is congested.

It'd be easier, yeah, easier. Have I ever found satisfaction in *easy?* There's no challenge in easy, no sweat, no adrenaline in easy.

One of our neighbors back in Akron planted plastic flowers. She wanted nothing to do with gardening or landscaping, so there they bloomed, bright and shiny silk replicas that slowly faded in the sun, jutting out of her garden. Last year, I planted a row of sunflowers from seed. My husband tilled the dirt with our friends' rototiller, turned the grass over into the topsoil, squeezed the throttle, pulled against the thrust of the blades that tried to run away with the dirt until the ground was loose, until it was ready for sowing. I pushed the seeds in, spaced them out and then hauled the hose around until I reached the garden. It's a long hose, two hoses connected together, and it's heavy, too, but I haul it (and that's what it is, a *heave*, a *ho*, a *haul*, like an *oomph*, a *grunt*, a *groan*) all the way to the edge of our property where I've planted these tiny sunflower seeds. And after they've gotten some water, a few days later or so, they sprout, and then I thin them so they have enough space to grow. More days, more water, more heaving and hoeing, some weeding, and they keep growing. They grow and grow, leaf out, form stalks as broad as baseballs, stretch as high as my head and then keep going, eight feet, ten feet, twelve feet, and I keep watering, keep weeding, even fertilize a little and then . . . then, as if there's nothing to it, there's a blooming head on top of each stalk, a huge blooming head of gold and yellow, tiny leaves of flowers bold and flashy, and I've done nothing at all to make them bloom, nothing, just watered them now and then, just a little maintenance here and there, and now, hundreds of seeds, thousands of seeds, sunflower heads as big as Frisbees, no, bigger, they are the size of open umbrellas, and my kids sit under them, marvel and laugh in wonder at them, this row of twelve-foot-tall umbrellas, and somewhere over the garden there's a pilot waiting for air traffic control to radio him in for a smooth landing.

Uprooted

❖

In our brick bungalow in Ashland, Brandon and I bought paint, buckets and buckets of paint for every room, for the doors and walls, for the cabinets and garage's siding. The house was a blank canvas of white and we needed color. He used the roller and I painted the trim and borders. We pulled up carpet in the kitchen and the bathroom, patched cracks with spackle, replaced electric outlets and light switch plates, upgraded ceiling fans and lamps, and installed new knobs and handles on the cupboards. We hung wooden shades from the windows to let light in during the morning and block the glare in the afternoon.

In the early summer months we lifted the bricks from the last owner's landscape borders and stacked them on the back concrete slab. We dug out the overgrown weeds, hacked at the arborvitae stumps until they were up and out of the ground, then smoothed the earth, spread and tamped down paver sand and arranged the bricks in staggered patterns. Around our newly formed patio, we planted holly bushes and the requisite transplanted daylilies and hostas. When the holly bushes were ripped from the landscape by an overeager coonhound-Doberman on a lead, we planted new shrubs, tried Russian sage that spread its broad and fragrant branches. I cursed and pruned the Rose of Sharon whose seeds are ridiculously fertile, sending hundreds of stubborn roots into my strategically planned landscape bed.

Even on our postage-stamp property, plants are reseeding and transplanting themselves, spreading their offspring wherever they can put down roots—Columbine, daylily, iris, hosta, Rose of Sharon—all expanding until there's nothing left to do but pull up the shoots, push a shovel into the soil, separate the bulbs and plant them elsewhere to begin the process over.

And here in the front bed, here at our home, the birch I planted is thriving.

Dad cut down their river birch. The landscape is different now, sunnier. Mom has planted her own Russian sage and butterfly bushes, rhododendron still present but surrounded by new growth and other transplants, daylilies and hostas, a limelight hydrangea I bought her that blooms prolifically. Still by the deck the climbing hydrangea stretches, flowerless, but the Japanese maple is making a comeback off of that one little shoot. I visit and survey the yard and the house for what else I might be able to take, what more I should leave behind.

The Seeds You Sow

In the mornings before I slip off to work, Henry, our third child, stumbles into the bathroom and asks, "Mom, can you snuggle on the couch with me?" This is our morning routine, me in dress pants and a blouse applying makeup, blow drying my hair, every other body in the house still warm beneath the sheets in darkness, and Henry in Minion pjs, groggy, picking through my drawer of makeup and brushes. "Are you ready yet?" he says.

"Almost," I say.

Before we settle on the couch, he asks for juice in his Pixar Cars sippy cup. "Let's snuggle now, Mom," he says.

"In a minute, buddy," I reply. "I need to make my coffee and get my breakfast ready."

The commute to my new job is an hour door to door, and if I make it out the driveway before seven, I miss some of the rush. There are mornings when I hope he stays asleep, my final child, so I can slip out early and maybe get to work early and then maybe get home early, but he's always been one to wake before the sun, no matter what time we put him down at night. He expects this time with me, alone, under the crocheted blanket on the couch. I sit down and reach for the remote; he crawls onto my lap, all forty pounds of him now, at age four, the weight of my world nuzzled underneath my chin. His wavy hair smells like sleep and summer.

"Put on Neck-flicks," he demands, but I opt for PBS, seeking every learning opportunity. *Martha Speaks* is almost over, and as *Curious George* begins, I sigh and start to shift him off my lap. I feel the minutes ticking away from seven, the traffic backing up along the interstate toward Cleveland, calculate what time I'm likely to arrive in the office and how long I will need to stay before I can log off and get back on the highway again, how that departure time will affect my arrival, my evening, a rush from road to

44

driveway to dinner to bath to bed. If I don't leave now there will be no time. I better hurry.

"I have to get going, buddy."

He presses down into my abdomen and pulls the blanket closer. "Not yet." Curious George is getting ready to sort a bunch of mixed up vegetable seeds.

I squeeze Henry to me and lift him off my lap, back onto the couch, and kiss his head. "See you later, buddy. I love you." He's engrossed again, both hands on his cup and staring at the TV. I gather my purse, my laptop, my mug, my cereal bowl and keys and head toward the door.

"Hey, you leaving?" Brandon calls from the kitchen.

"Yes," I say, "You startled me. I didn't know you were awake."

"Just got up. Have a good day."

"Thanks, you too. See you tonight. Love you."

"Love you too. Drive safe."

Henry is our compromise child, the last attempt to get pregnant again after our two older children were born, after two more miscarriages.

"I can't watch you go through this again," Brandon had said.

"Just one more," I said instead.

This chubby baby who never took a bottle because he didn't have to—I was always within reach, even at my desk where Brandon brought him to nurse every two to three hours when I worked within a minute's drive— Henry leaps off of the couch and full-speed runs toward me at the door. "Mom sandwich!" he shouts, hugging me as tight as he can and pulling Dad in with him. He puts my head between his hands, turning me side to side and plants kisses on each cheek. I kiss him back.

"I have to go, sweetheart," I say, "I love you."

He runs back to the couch. Brandon smiles and hugs me too, embraces me and my laptop and purse and cereal bowl and mug. "Bye, babe."

I back out of the driveway and watch the silence, imagine my house and its inhabitants entering this day as I leave, speed and brake and accelerate, *this is the life I want*, signal and yield and merge, *this is the life I chose*, away, away, away. Brandon makes himself a cup of coffee and settles in beside Henry. By the end of the half hour, I will be in the shadow of skyscrapers. By the end of the half hour, Curious George will have figured out the fruit that grows comes from the seeds you sow.

Somebody's Daughter

HEAVY DEW REMAINED ON fronds of corn in rows we picked at dawn. My father, brother, cousins, aunts, and uncles each took a row and raced to see who could fill their baskets fastest. Dad showed me how to pull away the harvest with a quick twist of the wrist, to feel the fragile kernels harbored safe inside for ripeness. I returned to my basket with an armful of ears cradled against my chest. Bright rays of sunlight arced between the trees and rose to burn away the dew, but we were already damp, our clothes soaked through.

The bushels filled to overflowing, corn piled high above the bed as we drove, bouncing down the path to lift each basket, a cloud of dust behind us. My cousins and I knelt on the tailgate, the sun above the tree line warm on our chapped hands and legs, minutely cut from blades of stalks in the aisles. *Fugmans are hard workers*, we were told, and we felt it in the burn of our muscles, the sweat under our clothes, the strain of our skin absorbing sun and dew, taking in these lessons by osmosis. It is the way we learned all things, the way—like seeds do nothing but receive the sun and rain and soil—we grew.

The truck pulled in front of the barn and we pranced off, skittering up the hill to where my aunts continued the harvest, lifting mud-stained tomatoes away from the vine, cutting the prickly fruit of cucumbers and zucchini into other baskets. We tiptoed through the tangled garden that started with so much order and now unfolded into chaos, pumpkin vines encroaching into zucchini hills, tomatoes resisting their cages and cascading over wires.

My aunt, who just an hour earlier walked the same muddy field as us, emerged from the blue farmhouse with her hair curled and styled, light makeup applied, a white button-down blouse and blue jeans on, her eyes sparkling, her smile ready for customers at the corner vegetable stand. One of seven brothers and sisters, she is the face of the farm. Like my father, she is long and lean, strong, able hands calloused but scrubbed clean.

"Can I go with you?" I asked, eager to stay with her at the corner underneath the red awning all day, to rake the dirt smooth after customers came and went, to bag their fresh tomatoes and jalapeños in brown paper bags, to collect their cash and calculate change. I wanted to be a businesswoman—an entrepreneur, like my mom and dad—I ordered jewelry and knickknacks from Oriental Exchange and set up a card table next to the corn. In between customers, I made string bracelets, polished dirt off of vegetables, drank Pepsi, and ate Doritos with my cousins.

On a slow afternoon when the sun beat down—all the families off at barbecues, all the fishermen out on Lake LaDue—no customers came. We were tired of sitting in the cab of the red pickup where the vinyl seat cushions stuck against our thighs. My cousins and I decided to skip across the street to the Auburn Inn for a burger. The streetlight changed green to yellow to red and then back again to green. We waited for a car to pass and then began to cross.

"He-ey!" a man whistled from the open window of the passing vehicle. I waved and grinned, called, "He-ey!" back.

My aunt shouted, "Sarah! You don't know that man! *Never* wave to a stranger." I blushed and finished crossing the street, a little faster dash than usual up the stairs and into the bar. The bartender knew us by name and took our orders. We sat on the barstools and spun back and forth while we waited, just a couple Fugman girls selling corn in Auburn Township on a summer day.

Auburn Township doesn't show up on Google Maps. It's just a few crossroads and "Auburn Center" where Old Route 422 crosses Auburn Center Road. Its 3,300 residents are 99 percent Caucasian and 1 percent "Other." The corner stand where my aunts sold vegetables each summer was a red tent awning erected in a dirt parking lot at the intersection of State Route 422 and State Route 44. Across the street was the Auburn Inn, where my dad and uncle could be found sitting on barstools most nights of my childhood. We were a township of loose zoning rules and farmers who served as trustees. Our social calendar revolved around family birthday parties, pig roasts, and clambakes, Memorial Day picnics and the Great Geauga County Fair.

One summer, Auburn launched its annual Fourth of July parade down Auburn Center Road, and I got to be in it. I was eleven or twelve. Mom spent the morning washing and polishing the semi that would pull a piece of excavating equipment on the carry-all behind it. A good percentage of the township's population rallied around the perimeter or rode in the parade itself, on the backs of the volunteer fire department's trucks, on motorcycles, and behind boom-boxes lifting pom-poms to music. Local business owners hung banners from the sides of their vehicles and waved while their kids threw candy out passenger windows to the patches of families huddled beside the road.

I'd be wearing my new bikini and cut-off shorts, waving and throwing candy with some of my parents' friends' kids to the crowd along the parade route. Each triangle of fabric was striped purple and orange and held together with a purple length of string, tied in back and around my neck. I had picked it off the rack and held it up for Mom to inspect.

"Please??" I had begged, ready to shop in the juniors section, ready to look so grown up. She hesitated, but the suit came home with one condition: Mom would modify the bottoms, pulling in the strings between the front and back pieces of fabric so they were connected.

I ran past Mom and the shiny, clean trucks in the driveway, past the vegetable garden and the edge of the field of corn just beginning to shoot up from the topsoil (not quite knee high by the Fourth of July), past my aunt and grandma weeding between tomatoes, and headed toward my dad's shop. Inside, layers of dust thickened on cabinets and equipment like river sediment. The garage doors were open at both ends to let a breeze blow through. I skipped over the concrete and oil spills buried in kitty litter to see if there were any Pepsis in the refrigerator. The rusty 1950s era Frigidaire Cycla-matic was decorated with dozens of bumper stickers that declared my dad and uncle's allegiances: STP and Valvoline, Go Army and Bill Elliott Racing Team, Let It Snow and Bowling Green National Tractor Pull, Miller and Coors, Ford and John Deere and Goodyear. I always hoped there would be pop inside, but usually it only contained twelve packs of Miller Lite, maybe the occasional half-full Gatorade jammed into the corner for one of the workers.

It was so hot, and I couldn't wait for the water hoses and squirt guns along the parade route to squirt me in my bikini and ponytail riding high on the back of my dad's trailer, waving and grinning. I was proud of my parents' business, proud to ride so high in the big equipment with their names stenciled in bright paint on the doors.

I pulled forward the tab of the Pepsi can and heard the crack and sizzle of cold carbonation, pushed and wiggled the tab until it broke free and then gulped the pop back. My cousins were collecting the tabs, so I did, too, pocketing this one in my jean shorts and dashing out the door into the bright summer sunlight, the triangles of my bikini wrinkled and flat against my chest.

❁

Today, the shop, as we've always called it, is a long and broad garage large enough to fit two dump trucks and their trailers end-to-end and side-by-side with space around the perimeter for tools, tractors, snowmobiles, and four-wheelers. Dad built the first wing of the shop in 1987 when I was five, on a patch of land just north of my grandparents' farmhouse. The business itself began in 1984, R&R Excavating ("R&R" for my parents' names, "Rose" and "Roger"), when I was two and the three of us were still living in the trailer park in Newbury. Back then, Dad stored equipment in a lean-to off of the old schoolhouse on my grandparents' property. He built the business one machine at a time, one invoice at a time, one basement or septic or driveway at a time, always imagining the next possibility to secure a future for his family, for his wife, for his sons, and for me.

The shop was the place Dad spent his evenings while my mom carted us from after-school practices home to work on assignments at the house, while my mom prepared dinner and we ate, sometimes with him but often without him, Dad still at the shop or down the street at the Auburn Inn or Patio.

The shop was a man's world, my dad's world, with drawers and towers and metal containers filled with washers and bolts and nails—who could ever use all of those washers? Why would you ever need to buy more?—rows of wrenches hanging from nails along the wall, toolboxes jammed with hammers. Amidst the metal and rust and dust is a sense of order, convenience, and strategy—everything has its place, everything is where you'd expect to find it, the awls with the awls, drill bits near the drills, Phillips and flathead screwdrivers together in one drawer.

But R&R Excavating had two "R's" for a reason. Dad's job was to remove dirt and shape the landscape. He created empty spaces to be bricked in or bordered or graded or paved over. Mom was human resources, accounts payable, and payroll, the work that filled in the empty spaces. I watched my mom enter codes into the computer, watched her wait for the mail to come. She brought order to the chaos of weight slips. She turned scribbled-on papers into invoices into dollars into gas and groceries and my new string bikini.

※

"Mom, could you send me some photos of the refrigerator in the shop," I ask via text message one night, "I can't remember what's on some of the stickers." The images arrive in my phone, front-ways and side-ways. I make note of the labels, some I remembered but most forgotten—Bowling Green National Tractor Pulls, Bill Elliott, STP, Valvoline—and then flick over to the second image.

There they are, underneath the yellow Little Rascals sticker, "Buckwheat says—life at the beach is o-tay!" There they are. The calendar girls. There are six of them tacked onto the fridge, as early as 1998 and as recently as 2009, six naked women hanging as part of six monthly tear-off calendars, a new girl for each month. Some of them are January's girl, one is May, and a couple made it all the way to December. They are named "Kendra" and "Michelle" and "Jen." They grin and twist, sulk and pout, breasts exposed or barely hidden, full wavy blondes windswept and sleek, oily bronzed brunettes with hair straight. One plays with her hair and teases the camera after having just loosened her top. Another looks into the distance aloof. Another presses her palms against her chest; underneath them her breasts are enormous, so large against her skinny frame I can't believe they're real, it just doesn't seem possible. Another is against a bedspread with her arms above her head, *I'm waiting*, she seems to say to the stranger holding her picture.

None of these women resemble the people in my family, but from the distance of two decades, I see a young girl in a bikini running through the shop, fabric triangles sliding on a purple string. She skips around the kitty litter covering oil spills to find a beverage she can drink in the fridge. Greasy boobs and smiles look down on her knobby knees and flat chest.

I can hardly fathom these women on the refrigerator. What are they doing there, then, now, still?

"That's somebody's daughter!" I shriek to my husband.

He laughs, "That's what men say after they've left a strip club, 'That was somebody's daughter I just threw dollars at.'" I stare at him. "Well, look,

I'm not saying it's right! I'm just saying that's what happens. That's the way men think."

❉

"I know how boys think," Dad said as we drove down Wing Road some summer day. We were headed to the Patio, or maybe the Auburn Inn, or maybe to deliver another picking of sweet corn to my aunt on the corner. "So be careful."

I didn't know how boys thought. Instead of Barbies, my brothers and I played Matchbox cars in our bedrooms upstairs, and I made up soap operas for them, pairing the dark colored cars with the yellows and pinks so they could be married while my brothers raced them around the braided rug track. An older boy taunted me once to reach between his legs for marbles he had hid there, and I reached, aware suddenly of a burning sensation in my gut, but the boy just grinned and moved them closer to his crotch, *Can you reach them now?* he said. In elementary school, Nick and Jason and Brett and Charlie chased my friends and me on the playground, and I ran so fast to the top of the slide and leaned over the rail laughing and teasing and shouting, *You can't catch me!*

Except that's what I wanted, all of those times on the playground. To be caught.

What does that mean, how boys think?

I nodded and stared out the window.

❉

For my thirteenth birthday, my cousin gave me a deck of cards, and as I opened them and splayed the deck, my face turned red. Every card had a picture of a naked man. I looked away. "I can't take these," I said, shocked and embarrassed, and handed them back to her. Jonathan Taylor Thomas, Awesome Bill from Dawsonville, and a broad shouldered quarter horse watched us from their pinned positions on the walls.

She laughed, "Oh, don't be ridiculous! I thought it was hilarious."

I doubt I'd ever seen a penis before, and if I had, it was the little nub of a baby boy's as I changed a diaper, certainly not the variety, size, and color of them in the deck of cards. It was a brief encounter burnt in my memory, those cards spread wide in my hand for just that second. Dicks. Lots of dicks.

Breasts, however, I had seen, barely concealed behind bikinis, bodies bent for angles, contours, and lines. I don't know when I became aware of the women hanging in my dad's shop or the moment it began to embarrass me to see those bodies on display. They were beautiful, flawless forms. They smiled. They pouted. They sulked. They weren't just on the refrigerator; they were on the walls next to innocuous posters of tractors, lined up with the machinery, like equipment you used and then abandoned.

But the men in my family love machinery. They buy old equipment and restore it, refinish it, retune it, rework it until it is running again, strap it to a trailer, and haul it off to an antique tractor show. The men in my family love their women, too; they'll hug and dance with a few drinks, they'll hold the suddenly fragile hand of their women after surgery, they'll spend long hours on the road with them, sit for long hours on the couch watching a movie with them. It doesn't surface the way it might in romantic comedies, but it's there, love, it's there. It might come out disguised as jealousy—don't flirt with her on a barstool, don't hover too close at a concert, unless you want to be cussed out, unless you want a fist in your face, unless you want a finger jabbed against your chest. Most of the time, love rumbles in by paycheck. Those men, they are the providers; they work and work and work, they bring home the bacon, they win the bread. The women prepare the bacon and the bread, they wash the jeans and sweep the clumps of mud out from under the rug.

The world my parents created for me was protected, innocent, and unexposed to the threats of the larger world. I grew up naive, incidents of dissonance just tiny blips on my radar of rural complacency, little sizzles of heat and friction where the silence cracked and broke, then froze over again. We listened to country music before it turned into pop country, before it was all beer cans and tailgates and girls in tight blue jeans, when it was still mostly storytelling. We weren't allowed to watch The Simpsons; instead we watched Looney Tunes and TGIF, Nickelodeon and Saturday morning cartoons, never anything R-rated.

The calendar girls didn't dance throughout the house; there weren't naked women tucked away in the bathroom, no *Penthouse* or *Playboy* or *Maxim* issues I was aware of. Nudity was uncommon. My parents came out of their bedroom fully clad in the day's clothes. As I stumbled into womanhood (it certainly never felt like a blossoming), Dad turned the other way when I emerged from the bathroom wrapped in a towel. We shielded ourselves. We did not look.

The women in my family wore clothes with buttons and collars and sleeves. My aunt—flowing white blouse and blue jeans, bright blue eyes and blonde hair—defined country beauty. Clothes were meant to clothe the body: bras were meant to strap the ladies in place, practical panties fully covered both butt cheeks. Not that I ever saw them *in* them; Mom pulled on her underclothes underneath a robe and did so magically, never revealing an inch of skin. I always thought she was beautiful no matter what hair style, no matter how stubby she thought her thumbs were, how deep the scar from three c-sections, or how crooked her teeth. In spite of these minor dissatisfactions that surfaced intermittently, she didn't spend hours in front of her mirror.

Maria, the mother of the three girls I babysat for, stood underneath the bright lights of her bathroom. The mirror stretched all the way across the wall, from the sink up to the ceiling. She flipped her hair over and dried it, flipped it straight and dried it more using a round brush for curl, then used the curling iron sizzling the ends under, sprayed a sticky mist around this masterpiece, then began the process of applying makeup. I watched her reflection in the mirror next to mine. The Sarah in the mirror had bad posture, a curl of bangs across a greasy forehead, and acne. She was Sarah-plain-and-tall, ponytail and oversized t-shirt, jeans and white Keds. I grimaced. I turned my gaze back to Maria in the mirror.

So many brushes and powders and shadows and tubes of lipstick, bins of clips, bottles of sprays and gels and conditioners and nail polish lining the long bathroom counter. It took forever until she was ready, a few final glances in the mirror, a few final assessments of her features. She looked beautiful, movie star beautiful, model beautiful, flawless. She flashed her brightest white, bleached teeth smile and somehow made her eyes sparkle. "All ready!" she sang.

I don't remember where she was going or who she was going with, but it was the middle of the day and the three girls and I jumped on the trampoline in their backyard. We jumped and bounced and tried to send each other higher into the air, reaching to touch the branches that overshadowed us.

The dress I bought for my first Homecoming dance my sophomore year of high school was black velvet with elastic bands that stretched like downward shining rays of the sun across my back. It clung to my body and extended all the way to the floor with a slit up to my thigh. It was soft and flattering. Of all the dresses I tried on it was the one I wanted most—sleek, elegant, mature, and nothing like I'd ever worn before, like a beauty pageant contestant or a Barbie.

As I rode with my mom to the hair salon in Mantua that morning, I wasn't thinking of the boy who would pick me up later. The stylist curled and pinned and braided and curled and pinned, then sprayed and sprayed again. My head was transformed into a royal crown of brown ringlets. I turned my head to the left and the right while the stylist held a hand mirror behind me so I could see the full effect of what she'd done. I was stunned.

At home, I slipped the stretchy black fabric over my head and felt it fall heavy down my chest, across my hips. Mom smiled, teary eyed, "You look so beautiful!" and I smiled back, unsure. I had seen myself reflected in plenty of mirrors. I had seen myself in videos dancing on a kick line where I felt sexy but looked gawky, long-legged, lanky, and lean. I didn't look anything like I thought I should; I didn't look anything like the way I felt inside—smart, friendly, insightful. I looked terrified.

Mike arrived in his dad's black pickup wearing a suit. I posed in front of the sweet autumn clematis in full bloom, its thousands of four-petaled fireworks open and fragrant on the breeze. I stood a little slouched, a little unsure, next to our black lab who blended into my dress. Then it was my dad next to me.

"You look beautiful, Sare," he mumbled under his breath. We posed together, my fingers interlaced in front of me, Dad's hands loose next to his dusty jeans, both of us smiling. Then I was by myself in front of the clematis, blooming fragrant. I popped my hip and turned to the side. I put my hand on my hip. I smiled at the camera, a woman, not a girl, put together and decorated and posed. I felt beautiful.

I borrowed my dad's truck to haul a grill for my ten-year high school reunion Labor Day weekend. After I lifted my two children into the backseat of the truck and then propelled myself into the driver's seat, I reached behind the steering wheel for the keys. There, just a bit to the right and down near the ground attached to the ashtray of pennies, hung a small calendar and a woman. She arched her back and looked straight at me, smiling broadly. She was topless and wearing a string bikini bottom. I blinked. *Really, Dad?* I thought to myself and pulled Barbara Big-Boobs from the ashtray, tucking her inside the glove box.

I wanted to throw her away. But that's Dad's property, Dad's business, not mine, his full-grown daughter with her growing family eager to ride in Pop-Pop's truck. There she was, hanging there for all the world and my children and my mother and me to see, just a smile and two breasts, thin waist, tan skin. Some body. Hanging from the ashtray of my kids' grandpa's truck.

My high school friends, Chad and Kurt, were waiting at Chad's parents' place. The three of us stared at the grill, then Kurt and Chad each took an end and lifted it into the bed. I launched myself onto the tailgate while the kids waited in the truck.

"We'll need to secure it," I said, "My dad left some bungee cords here." The guys watched as I hooked two shorter ones together and latched them to the holes in the bed. I went rollerblading with Chad once or twice, some summer day before we graduated from high school. I probably wore cut-offs and a tank top; I probably let my hair hang loose so it would blow in the wind; I probably blared a radio station loud as I pulled up in my parents' Thunderbird. I wasn't interested in dating him, but I wondered anyway whether he wanted me, whether he was attracted to me, whether he thought I was pretty.

The important thing about hauling anything in the bed of a pickup truck is to make sure the straps are secure against the body of the grill, wrapped all the way around the back and hooked in tight so it won't slide if you accelerate too fast. I have learned a lot from watching my dad these thirty years, not the least of which is how to keep things in place.

The next time I opened the passenger door to load my kids inside so they could ride around the farm with their grandfather, there she was again, her breasts large and exposed, hair full and suspended in a wind stream, bikini bottom bright. There she was again, out of the dark of the glove compartment and into the light.

"Well, I see Barbara Big-Boobs found her way out of the glove box," I said, unable to keep the edge of sarcasm out of my voice. Dad smiled bashfully. She might still be there, swaying slowly from the rim of the ashtray as they drive, my mom in the passenger seat, looking normal and healthy and beautiful, even with all of her clothes on. She might still be there, riding along with Grandma Rose and Pop-Pop.

My daughter is six and standing in front of the mirror with a long-sleeved maroon dress on her rail of a body, beautiful already with her loose blonde curls and blue eyes, joy leaking out of her pores. She is watching how the dress moves with her. She pulls the strings around the back tightly and says she likes it *that* way. How often have I hovered in front of the same mirror, turned my back to my reflection and then looked over my shoulder? Every piece of glass I pass, I glance toward that dark image to see if I can see what others see when they walk by me. To see if there's any beauty showing.

"Why?" I ask. She just shrugs and smiles and skips down the hall. I watch her and then turn to look in the mirror.

"Okay, now pucker your lips, I'm going to apply the lipstick," my cousin said. I sat on a chair in my bedroom with my head tilted up to meet her hands working on my face. She concentrated, smeared the stick carefully across my lips, mouth open wide. "Okay, press your lips together," she instructed. I pressed my lips together and moved my jaw to the left and right as I had done so many times with Chapstick. "Don't do that!" she chimed, "You should never rub them side to side like that. It smears the lipstick all over the place." She handed me a tissue and I blotted the color away.

I think about this every morning as I dot cover-up here and there with a powder brush, apply layers of eye shadow across my lids, brush mascara through my lashes, and then uncap my tube of magenta lipstick from Bare Minerals that declares in its name, Live Large, careful to only press my lips together, never side-to-side. I remember Maria in the mirror, the beautiful Maria and her bleached teeth and perfect hair and perfect makeup, and I look at myself sideways and long, stare into the blue of my irises and curse the turn of my nose again—*You must be a Fugman girl, are you Roger's daughter?*—morning by morning, practice a smile and a frown. I try to catch myself unaware that I'm looking in the mirror—what do I look like when I'm not trying to see?—then pucker up to my reflection. The lipstick is almost always gone by lunchtime, impressed upon my coffee cup, a thin line of color outlining my otherwise bare lips.

"You look nice," my husband says as I gather my things to go to work. He has just finished cleaning up after breakfast and will spend the day here at the house with our youngest son, Henry, playing Matchbox cars or trains, folding laundry, sweeping clumps of mud off of the kitchen floor.

"Thanks," I say with a smile. I step out of my Ford Fiesta in the mornings wearing black heels and gray dress pants, a scoop neck blouse and blow-dried hair. My Live Large lipstick is still bright. My heels click against the pavement. My hips sway. I smile. I am focused on the task at hand: walk to my office. Unlock the door. Type and call and answer and balance and promote. I'm all business. I'm all class. I'm professional. I'm success and confidence and charisma. Look at me. Look and look and look.

"Why do you always look at yourself in the mirror?" my now seven-year-old daughter asks as I ready myself for yoga class. Earlier she stared while I applied the powder and lipstick, then skipped away to ready herself as well. She has already crossed a line, from mimicking her mother's actions to innocently questioning her mother's behaviors.

"Because I want to make sure that everything's in the right place," I say, embarrassed. Why *do* I always look at myself in the mirror? There's a reason they call the dressing table a 'vanity.' What do I hope to catch here in this reflection, what façade do I hope to project—sexiness? professionalism? fitness? beauty? perfection? ease? self-confidence?—and what is it that my daughter sees? Does she see her mother, strong and clean and proper, like I saw my aunt after she worked hard in the field, fresh and beautiful? Does she see her mother, fit and lean and manicured, like I saw Maria in the mirror? Does she see her mother, v-neck blouse and tight blue jeans, the way I saw Shania Twain in country music videos, the way my mom might dress to go out for a drink with my dad? Or does she see her mother, insecure, obsessed with her appearance, her shallow secret showing itself in this daily ritual, unable to measure up to the calendar girls, unable to measure up to the women in the photo shoots and magazine racks, unconscious even that this comparison is happening, unfair internal comparisons against the Photoshopped images, façades themselves, glossy bodies embellished and airbrushed?

How long have I wanted to look good, to feel attractive, to be flattered and admired? How long have I thought this mattered, keeping up appearances, flashing a flirty smile, sculpting muscles, practicing a certain kind of walk, a certain kind of posture that would draw a certain kind of attention? In middle school I walked with my gaze down, slouched, the posture of uncertainty. As I marched with the drill team across the football field in high school, *Keep your chin up, smile, shoulders back, T 'N' A, ladies!* the captains called. We were synchronized young women with the same makeup, polish, and shine. It wasn't until a man was caught with a video camera at our practices, zooming in on legs and crotches, that we felt dirty, exposed, violated. As if we were just bodies, just bodies dancing for a camera.

In the morning, Lydia will come out of her bedroom and assess what I'm wearing. "Mom, we match!" she will say, and I will be proud and worried and happy that she wants to be like me. I will wonder how deep that desire is rooted, how much of it she will resist, what she will embrace.

"You aren't going to wear that," Dad said.

"Oh, Da-ad," I smiled, rolling my eyes and walking out the door. A thousand boys waited for me, parked in the silver hatchback or pulling up the driveway in a black or blue or purple pickup truck or sauntering down the asphalt walkways of the amusement park or pushing quarters into arcade slots or shooting hoops on campground basketball courts or running the carnival Ferris wheel or driving by the produce stand with a beep and a holler.

I waved, "He-ey!" no older than thirteen. I blushed with shame, but wasn't that the idea, wasn't that what this being a female thing was supposed to be about?

Later, the pickup boys would pull into the left-hand turning lane next to me in my Thunderbird, hoot and whistle, "Hey, baby! How about a ride?" I'd grin and stick my left hand out the window to wave *taken*, some other boy's promise ring prominent on my ring finger as if it meant forever already, and one of them said, "He doesn't have to know!" and my heart leapt in my chest and the light turned green and it was go, go, go, accelerating all the way up East Washington Street fast in my silver Thunderbird, so hot with the windows rolled down and the radio up and my hair blowing back and my tank top tight against my high school B-cup breasts.

The men who drive by and honk their horns, the men who whistle, the men who whisper "eye candy" and call you "grown-up," the men, the men, they are looking, they are watching, even now, they reach their arms around you and touch the small of your back as you talk, and you balk, and you walk away, startled and unsettled, but noticed. Yes, noticed, he *noticed* you, he's paying attention to you, he wants you. How long you've wanted to be wanted.

I know what those boys think. I see you, Barbara. I see you.

Genotype

WHEN I WALK INTO the Hitch'n Post gas station for a gallon of milk, the cashier behind the counter calls out, "You must be a Fugman . . . Are you Roger's daughter?" She recognizes the Fugman nose, or maybe the Fugman stride, or maybe the Fugman posture.

"Yes," I smile a Fugman smile, "I'm his daughter." I check out and head back to my car. I'm his daughter in both form and function. I bring home the bread and butter. It is me who sees the future just beyond my reach and swaggers toward it, ambition pressing its wet nose against my back and urging, *forward, forward.*

"Mom, can we go to the pool?" my kids ask, "Mom, can we go to the rec center?" my kids ask, "Mom, can we go to the park?"

I have time only for more, write more, read more, work more, do more until I flop exhausted on the couch with the remote. "Here," I say, "Why don't you watch a show?" Please leave me alone. I inhabit my own personal "shop," my skull its perimeter, my brain the spaces collecting dust and oil spills. It is the arena where I wander and wonder what others think of me. It is the place I huddle with a glass of whiskey and a laptop, contemplating the ways my dad was absent and ever-present in his absence, remote in hand and head tipped back, eyes closed. My children space out to *Looney Tunes* around me.

Even my hands, they are his, calloused like his in some of the same places, a blister flattened from the handle of a shovel or garden hoe, knobs along the top of my palm. His are enormous, swollen slabs, but mine are long and slender, feminine, different—the writer's bump on my middle finger, for instance. They were both made for work; they were made for pouring your sweat into the thing you love.

My children scamper in through the kitchen and hug my mother. I put the milk carton on the counter. We smile, delighted.

Genotype

"You look just like your mother; you two could be sisters!" people say when we're together.

I never could see it. I am my father's daughter. But here we are, words and phrases we keep tripping over, "Who's that one actor who plays that blind guy in that one movie?" Our eyes squint shut when we laugh, tears leaking. Looking even closer, yes, the shape of the eyes, like almonds, eyes the window.

Easy on the eyes, even, as one of my husband's friends said at our wedding, "Your mother-in-law is hot! Nice work," as if this is a prerequisite to finding a bride. Why not, I guess? Is there another woman I'd rather resemble? Mom, the gentle spirit, the comforter, the peacemaker.

It must be internal. The width of our hips for childbearing, the way I knew I might not be able to deliver naturally, just like her. The way I resisted going "all the way" with boys in high school because of her warning, because of her story—*got pregnant; too soon*—the way I carry guilt on my forehead. How I wanted to get married as soon as I was out of high school, or as soon as someone would have me, as soon as the current love of my life would propose. Marry young so I could begin my baby-making, my one true identity, the Mrs. I wanted to earn above any other degree.

Maybe the way we yearn for a certain kind of attention, a certain kind of love delivered in roses or compliments or quality time, the way our hopes rise. Maybe the way we default to silence, huddle up inside and wait for the storm to pass.

If we are eating dinner as a family and my husband is frustrated because no one is finishing their food or using their forks or staying in their seats, I am my mom, the lubricant, brake pad against rubber and metal.

My mom laments her flattened fingernails, fragile and thin. She keeps them filed low so they don't snag or break. She tucks her "ugly thumbs" inside her fists to hide them. Except when we garden together. We once reimagined an entire landscape centered around one tree. We moved mulch and dirt and fieldstones. We transplanted rhododendrons and roses.

We take the landscape we're given and transform it.

I touch the places on my palm where the tender places have hardened. There she is, there he is, and here I am.

II.

. . . humans can be made to infer the false belief that the blend of affection, fear, and desire which they call 'being in love' is the only thing that makes marriage either happy or holy.

— C.S. LEWIS, *THE SCREWTAPE LETTERS*

Someone's in the Kitchen

"Your desire will be for your husband,
and he will rule over you."

—*GEN* 3:16*B NIV*

AFTER A DAY ALONE with my children gardening, hiking, cleaning, coloring, singing, driving, or whatever we find time to do, we are sunlight, story, song, joy, we dance around the kitchen while we prepare a meal together. And then he comes in, their father, my husband, man as storm, angry at the driver who cut him off, who looked at him wrong when he passed him on the highway, and his team lost *again* and *I'm never watching another Sunday football game, not this season, this house is a wreck, clean up your toys, my back, my knee is killing me, I'm exhausted.* The sunlight is sucked out between screen door and latch, shades darken, shoulders tense, house shudders.

Or the day is its own storm without him as the source. He is gone and I am weary of whining children who steal each other's crayons and Matchbox cars and cling to my pants staring up with hungry, wet eyes as if I've never fed them dinner before and *please* prepare a meal for me, *will we ever eat again,* they beg, anything, everything, while I peel and slice the carrots, aware of the bright knife blade and cutting board, the swift and sure downward pressure that, should I turn too soon, could cut a finger, my own or theirs, or worse, and they are running, running through the kitchen, screaming and laughing, laughing and screaming, crying and whining, and I am still wearing my dress shoes, stepping over my toddler's toes in my sharp heels as he hangs from my pressed pants, presses his drooling, crying

65

face into the pressed pants I will have to wash and iron later after they are all asleep, praise God, asleep . . . and in the midst of this, he comes home from wherever he has been. He comes home, and he slides his arms around my waist and rests his chin upon my shoulder, nuzzles his beard against my neck, whispers, "I missed you."

Now, the cacophony recedes into the hum of afternoon as if the hurricane has passed, or we are paused in the eye of the storm, our children running laps around the house outside, his arms, oh his arms around my waist, his body close and I forget about the toddler hanging on my pants, forget the carrots and dinner, rest the knife on the counter, just for a moment while his beard is against my neck, his words slipping down my chest and into a reservoir that echoes over and over: *You are desired; you are adored. You are desired; you are adored.*

Yes, like it or not, he rules over you. You are an always gaping wound he can pour vinegar in or apply salve to but either way you want him and his attention on you. You put on eye shadow and rouge, choose the necklace that catches the specks of gold in your eyes and smile all the way through the flashy night with your slim figure in your clingy shirt and skirt that sways as you walk in that casual way as if you don't already know his eyes are following your every curve. Back in Paradise, you handed him some fruit and he took it, held the bushel basket as you plucked a perfect harvest from the tree. In Paradise, he lowered his hand to where you rested on the earth and pulled you up. You were not this cracked and leaking vessel then; you were his strength, his equal, his match. But then one slyer slithered in and said, *Are you sure that's what he meant?*

Now the garden is far, he is distant, labor is hard.

I am woman, not with but other, not equal but helper, no bone of his bone but splinter, thorn, dripping faucet of a wife who wants, yearns, aches, desires and therefore is ruled by *him*, Adam, man, who can give and give and give, or take and take and take, and still I will stand in the kitchen waiting to see which it will be tonight.

The Worst Soccer Mom

THERE MUST BE HUNDREDS of them, scattered all over the hill facing the field, men and women and grandparents and siblings sitting on lawn chairs and blankets. They've settled in with bags of Goldfish crackers, juice boxes, and hot cups of coffee they picked up at Starbucks. They chit chat with their hands tucked loosely in the pockets of their hooded sweatshirts, their weight on the left foot, then the right, then the left again, coolly observing their children. They recline.

I don't know any of the parents on the hill, don't recognize any of the boys, and my son is moving at sloth-speed along the perimeter of the practice field, a wounded, abandoned look on his face. My husband took him to his first practice on Tuesday night but he is out of town now and will be out of town for every Thursday night practice and Saturday game from here until the end of the season, all of eternity, really, and my son, Elvis, doesn't remember what his coach looks like, let alone her name. All I have is the team name. We showed up late after paying the sitter at 5:15, tracking down the soccer ball, shin guards, and cleats, running out the door only to run back in for the new water bottle we bought specifically for practice, shouting, "Hurry, hurry, hurry, sit *down,* close the *door,* buckle *up,* let's *go!*" shoving Lydia (six), Elvis (five), Henry (sixteen months), and the stroller into our tank of a kid hauler, then hurtling down every non-stop-light street in Ashland to make it to the soccer field. Late. The three teams of sixteen boys who started practicing at 5:30 each have a ball and are kicking it as hard as they can in every direction, except Elvis, who is lost along the sideline.

"Buddy, do you see your coach?" I yell from the top of the hill, shielding the sun glare with one hand where I stand in my Express dress pants and heels, which keep sinking into the dirt. Henry is strapped into the stroller and squirming. The hill is steep and I push the stroller along it, leaning against the slope so it doesn't tip over and tumble down the hill onto the practice field. Elvis is moping. All of the other parents look up from their lawn chairs at me and I smile and nod, gripping the stroller handle, imagining my hair frizzed out, purse slipping down my arm, shirt skewed slantways off my shoulder, bra strap sticking out. I'm not wearing glasses but if I was they'd be falling off my nose.

The kids started soccer practice two weeks into the college football season, when my husband travels each weekend doing production work for television. When I received the kids' practice and game schedule, I moaned. "Before games start," I complained, "We have two kids with two practices a week, and they each fall on different days—Monday, Tuesday, Thursday, and Friday." I waved the paper schedules about in the air in the kitchen, "And then, when the games start, the practices will cut back to two: one on Tuesday nights and the other on Friday. *Friday*. And *then*, the games are all on Saturday mornings. Do you know what this means??" My husband smiled, shook his head, and hugged me.

He knows what it means. It means *this* madness. This toddler-in-stroller or toddler-in-backpack, two kids who inevitably lose their jerseys fifteen minutes before we need to leave, madness.

"Is this team Aber's Towing?" I ask the nearest set of adults, who shake their heads at me. I keep walking, shouting down to the field, "Elvis! Move it! Find your coach!" And then he comes to a full stop and starts to cry. I let out an exasperated sigh and lock the wheels on Henry's stroller, tell Lydia to stay by him so he doesn't panic, and stride down to the edge of the field.

"Let's go, Elvis. Don't you remember who your coach is?" I am enormous and cast a long shadow over him.

He hangs his head and slowly shakes it back and forth, his lip curled in a long, empty frown. "We'll figure it out, buddy," I say, crouching down next to him along the sideline, feeling the eyes of parents everywhere, parents who got their kids to practice on time, husbands with wives who prepared snacks and packed drinks and brought chairs and invited grandparents, wives with husbands who are coaching the teams, the good and wise and stress-free parents who did not get out of work at five to come home to a house of unready children, unready to go anywhere, least of all to soccer practice.

"Does anyone know which field Aber's Towing is practicing on?" I shout.

Five- and six-year-old boys' soccer practice just started this week and I already hate it. Elvis doesn't even want to be here. He is switching between trying to balance his rear end on the soccer ball while the coach talks and concentrating on digging a hole in the sod with his cleat. He is running around the field with his hands in his pockets, playing with the quarters and dimes I didn't know he brought with him, flipping the boundary markers back in place when the ball goes out of bounds. While Lydia gets her cleats and sprints from the car to the practice field each week, ball in hand, all he really wants to do is squeal, chase, elbow, and shove his teammates. My husband and I probably signed him up too early; he's likely the youngest on the team and a head shorter than the rest of the boys. He could have done all of this at home.

Henry pushes against the stroller tray and whines. I'm out of Cheerios.

It isn't that I hate sports. When I first met my husband, he was the athletic director at a small Christian school in Northeast Ohio. On weekends during the year we dated, Brandon asked me to run the clock at the scorekeeper's table and quickly taught me to watch the ref and listen for his whistle, how to set the timeout clock and when to press the buzzer. He coached the varsity basketball team and in between plays, reassured me when I turned red as the crowd yelled about the clock or score being wrong. During one contest, the clock box stopped working and as men screamed at me from the stands, my now-husband got on the loudspeaker, calmly asked for patience and then said, "Relax, people. Read your Bible." He was reprimanded by the principal later.

When I wasn't behind the bench, I went to every game I could, in between classes and seasonal work, sat with each muscle in my body clenched as he yelled at refs, called time outs, encouraged his team, and threw the occasional clipboard.

It was easy to be swept away by the energy and excitement of a basketball game, the constant motion, the buzz of parents and family members watching the back and forth from offense to defense. They tabulated the minutes that passed since their kid had the ball last, since Coach pulled him out and sat him down, since the other kid got put in the game. If the team was behind, it was because the point guard wouldn't pass and no one would set up a screen so their son could shoot. When the ref missed a foul, they threw up their arms, *Are you blind?* They yelled, *Pass him the ball!* they yelled, *Box out!* they yelled, *Rebound!* they yelled, *That's a terrible call!*

These kids weren't *my* kids, but they were my boyfriend's team, and when the intro music played and the announcer called in each student athlete, my heart swelled. I loved to watch the way he moved on the court, the way he was always thinking ahead, encouraging, teaching, pushing, and improvising. He demanded respect in his dress pants, sweater vest and tie but approached each student athlete like he was his brother or son, draped an arm around a shoulder or back and leaned in to embolden a weary guard. The same caring coach erupted at a ref immediately after a foul call, threw up his hands and boomed so every soul in the gymnasium could hear. It was for the benefit of his team he yelled, but it made me shrink in my seat. It was his mission as a coach to light a fire in them, to make them want to win and teach them how to do it as a team. Being the girlfriend of this athlete and coach made me proud, even if entering the sporting world felt like learning a language for a country where they speak in whistles and flags.

I've never known this kind of passion, this intensity of competition. I was in marching band and drill team in high school. I read books for fun. My blood pressure is a steady one hundred over sixty. There aren't many things I get fired up about. But for Brandon, competition is a driving force in his life. Each season since we met has been defined by sport. I just want to have a good time; I just want everyone to have a good time, and if that means I don't try as hard at Scrabble so he can win . . . well, okay. Now we're all happy . . .

The closest I come to understanding the team concept are memories of practicing drills on the football field, except there was no team strategy, no last-minute shift in plans, no timeout to draw up a new approach. We marched into the stadium, marched onto the field, and marched into the stands. Then, we adjusted our hats and plumes, rested our instruments in our lap and gossiped for a quarter. A group of lanky brass players yelled, "They threw in the yellow hankie!" We startled to attention when the bass drummer beat one-two-three-four and the snare drum signaled instruments *up!* into the fight song. Apparently, we scored a touchdown. To compete, we chanted, "We've got spirit, yes we do, we've got spirit, how 'bout you?" and every Columbia blue-clad band dork in white gloves pointed across the field at the opposing team's band, waiting for their response. "We've got mo-ore, we've got mo-ore!"

There was a score, but it was measures of musical notes. There was a drill, but it was a rigid eight-to-five march, turn at the bridge, count and play and march and count and play and listen for the staccato rap-tap-tap of the snare, watch for the raised wand of the conductor. No opponent's tuba player charged from the sideline to blast the bass drummer or intersect the trumpeter, there was no piccolo stand down on the forty-yard line to see who could trill the longest. We just . . . played.

❋

Brandon and I practice soccer with Lydia and Elvis in the backyard on weekdays during soccer season. My workday is over and dinner is smoking on the grill. We set up vague goals between the playhouse and our neighbor's cherry tree, the opposing goal between the ten-foot stretch of grass that separates our houses. Brandon passes the ball to Lydia and Lydia giggles and prances and I giggle and prance to defend her and Elvis giggles then grumbles then pouts. Eventually Elvis slumps off to the garage to find a tractor or dump truck to push in the sandbox. Brandon and I take turns blocking Henry from his tenacious attempts to waddle around the side of the house and into the street. As we kick the ball, Brandon gives Lydia some tips and encouragement, and we all cheer when she scores. She is elated but soon tires of soccer, skitters into the garage for her golf clubs, then her baseball glove, then her basketball.

Elvis and Henry squat next to the sandbox, maneuver die cast tractors and equipment, pour the piles of grit from one hill to a bucket to another corner and then back. Brandon calls to Elvis, "Hey buddy, you want to play basketball with us?" and he shakes his head, pushes the claw of the excavator into the sand. Brandon shakes his head and turns back to where Lydia is waiting to learn how to use the backboard to shoot.

I love watching Brandon with the kids on afternoons like this. During the summer, when he's home more, they take long bike rides and chase each other on the playground. They shoot hoops or kick or throw or hit balls back and forth and laugh, he is the Tickle Monster in the living room, he is "it" on the playground and nearly knocks himself unconscious under the spiral slide; he is on his belly on the floor pushing cars and building Lego sets or assembling the Thomas train tracks for the hundredth time, lecturing the boys for taking it apart, again. This time during the summers and in the rare days when he is home is golden. I know how much fun they are having, my children and my husband. This is important to him. This is important to them. This is important to me.

And now I am at Lydia's first basketball practice. I'll refrain from going into all of the details about chasing Henry up and down the hallways, blockading him from trying to run onto the basketball court, laughing at him as he threw a mini-tantrum on the floor, and restraining him while he screamed and cried in my arms because he was tired. I also won't mention how the parent meeting was supposed to take place at seven o'clock but the speaker didn't show up until 7:25, so I could have darted out with both boys until it was time for the parent meeting instead of trying to manage the overtired toddler in the peripheral vision of all of the other parents with their perfect younger children sitting so obediently by their sides, or the other parents who have one perfect child, and that perfect child is on the court practicing, or they left their crazy nineteen-month-old at home with someone else, maybe a grandparent or a sister or a dad.

Brandon is out of town, again. T.S. Eliot was wrong, it isn't April that's the cruelest month, it's December, because that's when football and basketball overlap, when my husband works basketball games on Tuesday nights and leaves Thursday for a college football game somewhere out of state and then returns on Saturday night or Sunday. December is when I foolishly forget about soccer season and indulge in fantasies about my orderly family arriving on time to weekend sporting events, sitting attentively and cheering when a sibling makes a move or simply sitting still so I can clap with pride, clamp my palm against my chest to keep it from bursting with delight.

I want this to be fun. The optimist in me knows that it has the potential to be fun, and then nights like this happen and I watch myself yell and stomp and scream like I'm just a smidgen older than my nineteen-month-old, and then all three children are crying because Mom was mean and asked them to buckle their seatbelts so we could leave, so we could be *on time* because that's important, and please just get into the car, sit *down,* close the *door,* buckle *up,* let's go . . .

It isn't that I hate sports. I really like baseball and basketball, football and volleyball, tennis and golf. My brothers and I played backyard baseball all summer long. The tall spruce in the front yard was second base, and when we reached it, we called in a ghost runner to take our place. I threw pop-ups to my brother in the side yard, and he sent them sailing back. Since then, I've played summer softball with girlfriends from church and golfed on autumn afternoons with my husband, whacked a tennis ball with a racket under lights. Date night was varsity basketball games or hot Sundays around a doubleheader baseball diamond. The two of us drove to Cleveland on summer days to sit along the third-base line and watch the Indians lose, like they do. I navigate the bleachers in Kates Gymnasium at Ashland in order to find a bench long enough for the five of us to sit to cheer the girls basketball team through an undefeated season, the kids most ecstatic when Tuffy the Eagle makes an appearance. On Sundays in the fall after lunch, the kids playing a game outside or in the basement, Brandon and I recline on the couch, snooze along while the Browns lose, like they do.

And when my husband is out of town, sometimes I'll even venture out to attend a Saturday football game, watching the scoreboard from the Little Tikes playground as twenty toddlers and elementary aged girls squeal and run. I cheer when the quarterback makes a successful pass, mumble *They threw in the yellow hankie!*, anticipate the cannon's boom and my youngest son's sudden wail at what he didn't know to expect. I escort the kids back to our seats to watch the halftime show, the part I know best, and then it's time to go, our patience for sitting still expired and my willingness to watch from the playground over.

But when my husband is out of town, and I have to set my alarm clock on Saturday mornings so that I can take my three children to soccer games or basketball games in which at least one child whines for a snack or cries because he's too cold or bored or wants to run across the court to get the ball and won't sit on my lap, and when I forget the drink or snack or forget that it's picture day, or forget the water bottle or cleats or hair twisty or which way the shin guards go, or we're running late and one child won't put on his shoes or coat and takes twenty minutes to get out the door . . . well, then I hate sports.

I've been trying to figure out *why*, exactly. It isn't the sport. It isn't the noise. It isn't that I live in a town without family, with friends whose kids are unborn or younger, swinging this sport-thing, kid-thing, weekend-thing alone. I hate sports on mornings like these because they make me feel incompetent. They expose the side of me that isn't sharpened and honed, that isn't professional and collected. They reveal the skillset I lack: no one is impressed with my resume on Saturday when I forget the snack. No, I am not actually perfect; no, I cannot actually do everything, like I try to do. No, this isn't fun, and I hate that you are seeing me this way, I hate that I am back in middle school with my greasy hair pulled back in a high ponytail, glasses sliding down my nose, braces protruding from a nervous grin because *I'm fine, I'm fine, all is great, can't you see I'm okay and happy and fine?*

I keep thinking that next season will be better. Soccer is coming again in the spring. Brandon will be traveling, again, and lately my sanity has been leaking out from underneath the lid of my travel coffee cup. I keep sipping at it, *slurp slurp* but it just keeps dripping. It's only one season, and baseball is right around the corner, in the summer when it's warmer and sunnier and brighter and my husband is home more, here to coach their team, and I'll become one of the perfect parents, the coach's wife, a role I know, and I'll only need to bribe Henry with snacks, keep Henry contained on a blanket or chase him down the left-field line, and maybe I'll even have time to change out of my dress pants for once, into something more suitable, like jeans, like a t-shirt, maybe pull my hair back into a high ponytail and smile.

Brandon and I stand in the kitchen and watch the kids playing in the yard from the window. Brandon runs his fingers through his hair.

"I know this is going to sound weird," he says, "But the other day, I was thinking about how *mad* Elvis makes me, how slow he is to get ready, how he doesn't respond when I ask him questions, and I swear God said, not out loud or anything, 'He's not a little Brandon. Stop trying to make him into a little Brandon.'"

My husband wipes his eyes. I wrap my arms around him. I doubt that Elvis will play soccer this spring. He will run around the yard dressed as a cowboy or Superman, assemble Star Wars Lego sets, collect a bag of cars and run them across the carpet, play tag with the neighbors' kids, giggle and squeal and then push tractors in the sandbox until someday, maybe he'll ask us if he can play baseball or soccer or golf, or maybe, maybe the trumpet, maybe the drums, the piano, sit quietly in a corner with a pile of books, push a pencil across paper, whatever, son, whatever your heart desires.

At the last basketball game of the season, the announcer asks us all to stand and honor two of the fathers in the audience, who just returned from a year of military duty. The crowd applauds and they smile shyly. Afterward in the team meeting, the coach chokes back tears and says, "Two of our girls got their daddies back this week," and now I'm crying. I look around at the women I haven't paid much attention to before, women who have been coming to these practices and games all along, usually with a daughter or son on their lap or playing a game in the corner, women who have looked calm and content, like they have it all together, the women who are now standing beside the husbands they've seen over Skype, emailed, or talked to by telephone exclusively, for twelve months. *Twelve months,* I think, when I have my husband every six days or four days or three, or for three in a row and then five in a row and then one.

They are quiet, modest women with military t-shirts and jackets and bumper stickers. They are women who cart their children from one activity to the next, alone, sometimes arriving on time and sometimes late, sometimes showered and sometimes not, sometimes with makeup but most of the time, no. They have been keeping it together, alone. They are grinning now, an arm draped loosely over their children's shoulders and the other snug around their husband's waist, and there in the middle, they cling to whatever they can to carry them through these lonely days.

I look around the room of parents. Suddenly I *see* them. The grand-parents who are there each week I realize are with their recently divorced daughter. The mother next to me just got off the night shift. The mother in another row has a husband who drives trucks for a living, leaves at six in the evening and returns the next day at eleven to sleep for five hours, see his wife and their kids, and then leave again. As Henry arches his back against the floor and cries, their stares now feel a little bit more like mercy and a little less like judgment. Suddenly I am not so alone.

I set the Saturday alarm and showered even though I could've slept a little longer under the warm comforter. Before the game, I packed a purseful of dried cranberries and cashews because they both take forever to chew and aren't as filling. I tossed in two bananas for good measure. Thirty minutes before it was time to go to the game I told the kids to get dressed. Twenty minutes later we were still looking for Lydia's shorts, and Elvis was still in his pajamas picking at his toenails in the hallway while Henry waddled to the bathroom to splash his hand in the toilet. I almost lost it, but then the shorts turned up in a basket in the basement, Elvis had clothes on and just needed to find a coat, and Henry was following me around with his shoes. I corralled them into the entryway and tabulated the arsenal—jogging stroller, DVD player, snacks, water bottle, canned goods for the food drive, tennis shoes, Leapster, purse, cell phone, car keys—and someone was whining about bringing a toy for the ride, but it's ten minutes down the road. We trudged out into the snow and loaded up accompanied by the usual pre-game lecture—sit *down,* close the *door,* buckle *up,* let's *go*—and backed out the drive to the game.

Henry wanted to walk into the gym, so I let him. Elvis carried the Millennium Falcon in and set up camp with Han Solo and Luke Skywalker on a chair in the corner while Henry marched up and down the carpeted ramp until the game began, and then I wrestled him into the seat. When he started to arch his back and whine, I asked him, "You want a cookie?"

He said, "Yeah," and relaxed long enough for me to snap the buckle shut. The game began, Lydia hustling up and down the court defending when she was meant to defend and working to get open when the ball was in a teammate's hands. Because technology is amazing, I called my husband via Skype while he worked in the TV truck in some other city, and he watched his daughter dribble, defend, and shoot from his computer.

"I wish I could be there," he said, over and over.

I slipped Henry some cranberries and a couple of cashews throughout the hour, and when it was over, my heart rate was still normal.

"We'll call you later. I love you. See you tomorrow," I tell my husband through the camera on my phone.

We survived another hour of competitive sports. It was fun. We made adjustments.

Traveling with Donkey

ON THE WEEKENDS I travel with Brandon and leave behind our three children with my mom and then his mom after coordinating pick-ups and drop-offs and departures and arrivals and soccer practices and game cancellations, I find great satisfaction in doing nothing. I search for Panera Bread in Google Maps and drive towards it. I sit for long hours in restaurants reading or writing or browsing Facebook and Twitter, then drive aimlessly with the radio turned high through the city's main streets and then along mountain back roads. I do things I wouldn't do at home, like get a manicure and pedicure, or go to the local mall and try on clothes and maybe even buy a pair of silver embroidered jeans, bedazzled on the pockets. The day stretches from dawn to dusk without speaking to a single person.

We stay in hotels that give us a warm cookie when we arrive, or hotels that claim to stuff layers of heaven between the box spring and the fitted sheets, and no one argues because, wow, have you ever slept in one of those beds? With all of those down pillows and that down blanket and those soft sheets with the thousand-something thread counts? It *is* like heaven, especially when there are no children to wake you up before you're ready and your husband slips out of bed as quiet as can be for his five in the morning call time so that you can curl up inside heaven until your body just can't handle any more uninterrupted sleep, and you stretch, ahhhh, is it morning? I can't really tell because the room darkening shades are so good at what they do, so I open one eye with caution to sneak a peek at the alarm clock, which flashes something like eight or 8:30, much later than any *normal* morning back home, where the alarm chimes at 6:30 if one of our three children hasn't already shaken me awake with "I have to go potty!" or "Mom! Dad! Dad! Mom! Wake up!" Instead of getting out of bed, I prop a few down pillows behind my head and place my appropriately named laptop on top of my lap to indulge in three solid hours of research and writing, and it is *so good*. So good.

Some women might find this life on the road to be dull and lonesome, but if we were childless and my career allowed for it, I would travel with Brandon every single weekend. I cherish every quiet hour in the hotel room, the Do Not Disturb tag swinging slowly on the knob, as I type away or fall selfishly and guilt-free into whatever book I'm reading. Just when I've exhausted my creative energies is about the same time I realize if I don't leave soon, housekeeping won't come to refresh our towels and remake the bed (they *make* my *bed*). My stomach starts to growl and I realize I've skipped both breakfast *and* lunch, and now it's almost time to go meet my husband, so I grab a quick snack and anticipate dinner at a steakhouse or seafood restaurant with wine pairings or bourbon selections that will send this already successful day spinning toward perfection, playing footsie with my husband under the table and then retreating to that haven of heavenly bedding after we've ended the night singing "Jackson," like Johnny Cash and June Carter. That's what we do, all night long, laughing at each other and being a couple, a married couple without the distractions of duties or obligations or responsibilities, just for this weekend or this night and this moment, free to let loose and be ourselves, together.

My husband contracts with ESPN during the fall to work stats on the Saturday noon game on ESPNU. I pretend that I know what that means when I explain to my friends where he is each weekend—working stats on the Saturday noon game on ESPNU, of course.

"No, where *is* he," they ask again.

I blink, "Oh! You mean what city is he in?" I have to think a while before I remember, and almost always I guess correctly—Miami, Florida; Virginia Tech; Morgantown; Pitt; sometimes something on the West Coast or in the Mountain Time Zone. Those are always the hardest games. Remote cities require strange connections and a couple hours' worth of a time change for a couple stressful days of work.

I know that his work is in a climate-controlled TV truck with lots of video equipment and monitors and mostly men who queue up graphics and stats and trigger camera shots and replays and cuss occasionally/frequently/always if something doesn't time up quite right. I know he enjoys his work and that he has acquired the nickname "Donkey" because a

Producer (or Director, or one of his other six bosses) couldn't remember his name in passing and said, "Hello, Donkey!" and so, it stuck. My husband, Donkey. Somehow it seems just right.

When I travel with him, his coworkers express their condolences that I have ended up with this guy, "How do you put up with him?" they tease, and I grin. I also know that he is good at his job, whatever it is exactly that he does, because they keep asking him to do more of it.

Which of course I think is a good thing.

Natural Habitat

Camp Sandusky

AFTER THE BISON STUCK their long, muddy snouts fully through the rolled-down windows of our Ford Expedition and the kids shrieked with glee, we rolled up the windows and watched a sheet of rain advance toward our car. Brandon and I looked uneasily at each other.

"It wasn't supposed to storm today," I said, trying to pull up the radar on my phone, "Maybe it'll blow through quickly." But the sky to the west looked black with rain. It dripped and dribbled and then dumped onto the truck, our wipers whipping the water off of the windshield. "At least we did all of the outside activities first," I said over my shoulder to the kids.

The morning was filled with camel rides, monkeys, and Henry terrified by the spitting alpacas. After a quick sack lunch at the African Wildlife Safari Park, we drove through the "safari" part of the park, Brandon and I taking turns holding the feed cup out the window as the passengers of our car giggled. Most of the animals in the park are endangered species, and none of them are native to this region of Ohio. Reindeer, alpaca, bongo, Sika deer, llamas, Scottish Highlanders, and bison wandered freely through the overgrown grasses and dust, in front of and around the line of cars, hoping to grab a nibble before the rain came down. Their offspring trotted close by, and we imagined the alpaca parents explaining the daily operations, "You see, kids, when the doors open and the metal people-carriers approach, trot up and smear your noses against the glass until they stick out the nuggets of food. Some of them have *carrots*." We rounded the bend toward the final drive-thru exhibit of giraffes and zebras when the rain started.

Now the rain poured down and the sky blackened. We emptied the remaining nuggets of feed onto the ground and tossed the cup in the garbage bin at the exit. The outdoor temperature reading on our truck dropped from the low-nineties to mid-sixties over the remainder of our fifteen-minute drive. We took Route 2 at a minimum speed while the rain formed temporary rivulets across two lanes. The rearview mirror reflected the clouds in the west, flashing with lightning.

"What if there's a tornado?" Lydia asked. Elvis worried with her.

"There won't be a tornado, guys," I said, glancing sideways at Brandon in the driver's seat and then back at the rearview mirror, "You're safe. You have nothing to worry about."

The campsite was about five miles down the interstate, just past the exit for Cedar Point. The kids were all still too young for the amusement park . . . at least the part of the park we were willing to pay for. I found our campground through Groupon.com, a daily discount email. The African Wildlife Safari Park had been listed in the same email, and it seemed like a brilliant way to spend a few days—visiting animals and then camping with the kids.

It was still pouring as we exited the highway. The GPS lady announced, "Turn right at the exit. In five hundred feet, your destination is on the right." *Five hundred feet?* I thought to myself. *That can't be right.*

We pulled into Camp Sandusky. A crumbling asphalt basketball half-court with a rusting hoop of chain-metal net leaned toward the earth as if gravity itself were bringing it down, the court sagging into the dirt. A large corporate for-sale sign was staked into the front lawn.

"This doesn't look anything like the website," I told Brandon. He laughed under his breath.

It was still pouring. Brandon put the truck into park and slowed the windshield wipers to a more moderate pace. We could see the pool tucked behind the campground's general store. It looked clean but smaller than I expected, and no kiddie pool. To the right stood rows upon rows of cabins, ten-by-ten garden sheds with two windows and a door.

"Those sure look rustic," I offered. The highway roared to the right. I had no idea the campground was so close to the road. I should've looked at a map before making the reservation. But who imagines a campground right next to the highway? "Maybe our cabin is a bigger one."

We still had about a half-hour until check-in at three o'clock. I wasn't sure if we could back out of our reservation, but given that the coupon was for twenty-five dollars, it didn't seem like the end of the world to abandon our plans and drive home with some disappointed kids, maybe catch an afternoon movie at the dollar theatre until the rain stopped.

"I think it's slowing down," Lydia said. "It won't be that bad. Can we go to our cabin now?"

I smiled as the wind drove the rain into the side of our car. Lightning flashed again. Lydia is her mother's daughter. *It's just a little rain, pitter-patter pitter-patter, this is fun, look at it come down!* Together, we're always able to find the rainbow even when there wasn't one, the blackest sky alight only by jabs of electricity. Brandon and I continued to try to refresh the radar on our phones but couldn't get a signal.

"Well, what do you want to do, Sarah?" Brandon asked. I had imagined twenty-four hours of hiking, picnicking, swimming, grilling, and roasting marshmallows around the campfire. I had imagined a bright sun, a kiddie pool, reclining in a patio chair with a book and a bottle of water, my kids splashing and laughing. I had imagined casually tossing a football back and forth with my family, nothing but the sounds of nature as a backdrop. I had not imagined the highway roaring behind the campground. I had not imagined sheds. I had not imagined mud. I had not imagined a fallow cornfield and no trails. I sighed, avoiding Brandon's question and pressing update on my phone again, hoping this time the radar would appear with a forecast bright and clear of rain.

Vacations generally do not turn out the way I envision them. I don't know how these fantasies about what a family vacation ought to look like got planted in my brain; just because it is a vacation does not mean that the family members all turn into optimistic, adventure-loving, starry-eyed explorers. No, a family vacation simply removes the natural habitat of the cranky, the lazy, the whiny, the optimistic, and the determined-to-have-an-amazing-time, and dumps them together into another habitat to continue operating within their default setting. Together, the varying species trot around the feed truck and wait for meals, pressing their snotty noses against the glass and whining, "When is dinner? What are we having? I'm bored!" I should know this by now. With as much evidence as I've accrued over the last thirty years, I do not know why I expect otherwise.

After childhood birthdays spent in a tent or camper with my family or carsick in the back seat driving from one tourist trap to the Hoover Dam, after driving through Yosemite National Park and only stopping briefly to

peer over the edge of all sorts of scenic overlooks but never actually hiking into the wilderness we viewed from the window of our rented minivan, after passing the putt-putt golf course and maze castle back and forth
from the Daytona race track to the cabin with the cockroaches and yard of
rotting oranges, after driving for three days to vacation for two and then
turning around again to go home, after leaving the Outer Banks a couple
days early because there's nothing more to do at the beach, after watching
for Dad to arrive late Friday night to camp with us for the weekend, after
stopping every exit along the interstate until we found the one hotel with
vacancy . . . oh, after all of these things, and more, why should I expect
anything except craziness, disappointment, and utter disasters of vacations
we can all laugh at with abandon, at the safe distance of at least five years or
so down the road?

"You remember the time we drove to the Hoover Dam on your birthday making 'dam' jokes the entire way?" Dad laughs. "'You kids ready for
the *dam* tour?' 'Where can we get some *dam* bait?'"

I never miss my cue, "Can you *please* stop with the damn jokes already?" Good times. Fun times.

West Branch

Last June, we set up two campsites with my side of the family as a cold wind
whipped across West Branch State Park's lake, blowing heavy bursts of rain
through the trees that lined the shore. My brother and his wife and my
mom and dad shared one camper and Brandon and I and the kids shared
another, parked side-by-side along the lake. Lydia was six, Elvis almost five
and Henry just over a year old.

It had been four years since our last attempt at a family vacation with
my side of the family. The Great North Myrtle Beach Vacation Disaster,
when my stay-at-home husband and mild mannered mom set out around
eight o'clock Friday night to drive through the night to North Myrtle Beach
in our van with over 180,000 miles on it, and our kids took turns screaming
all through the night, and Mom had to hold a blanket up over the window
so the streetlights wouldn't keep our infant son and toddler daughter awake.
I had just come off of maternity leave and didn't want to take an unpaid
vacation day, so instead of driving with them, I worked the two extra days
at my new job and planned to meet Brandon at the airport Tuesday night.

Except, Bambi jumped in front of Brandon's van on his way to pick me
up from the airport. Bambi survived, staggered off the road, and ran into

the brush. The van staggered down the road and stopped, the hood caved in. When we finally rolled into the two-bedroom condo, our kids woke up and wouldn't go back to sleep the entire night.

The next day, Mom and I walked the beach with Lydia toddling in and out of the surf, and Mom said, "I'm worried about Brandon. He gets so *angry*. I can't imagine he'd ever do anything, but . . . do you think the kids are safe?"

I nodded, aware how hard this transition had been for him and also kind of stunned that my mom thought things were that bad. Were they that bad?

My dad and brothers arrived in time for Thanksgiving and then prepared to leave again on Friday, and I exploded about how *this always happens! you always leave early! can't you just relax, can't you just enjoy our company, my kids, my husband, our family, me?* unable to see the irony of my rant and my own late work-over-vacation arrival. We drove home in a rented minivan because our own van was not yet repaired from the Bambi incident, and a week later Brandon flew back to Myrtle to pick up our van with the repaired but not painted hood. It was the most expensive "free" trip we'd ever taken. And then my mom's dad died ten days later.

Not enough time had passed for us to joke about that trip. It hadn't quite lost its sting.

My youngest brother, Phil, had a blowout fight with my dad earlier in the week and had no intentions of joining us at West Branch that weekend. As usual, I was holding out hope for a grand time, remembering my own childhood camping trips with my parents and brothers, riding our bicycles on pathways carved by raccoons, swimming in Punderson Lake, playing rummy, catching fish with my grandpa, making hobo pies with Mom, and Dad telling stories around the campfire. Dad's suntanned face creased around his eyes as he guffawed, the fire bright and hot on the bottoms of our soles.

Those hopes gradually dissolved in the rain as my dad doused our firewood with lighter fluid. We huddled under umbrellas and hooded rain jackets around the ring, our teeth chattering, the kids chittering excitedly inside the camper, not sleeping.

In the morning, my mom and I cooked eggs and bacon over the lighter-fluid fire, still battling the chilly air, intensified by the lake.

"This figures!" I muttered. "We can't plan anything. It's freaking June, sixty degrees out, and gusting like a hurricane." The leaves of trees danced silver and green in the wind. Brandon kept his "I told you so" to himself while our kids watched a movie on the portable DVD player in the camper.

My dad and Bill got in the truck, "We're going to go get Phillip," they grunted, "and some fishing rods. And worms."

The rest of us took the kids to the playground and marveled at how much warmer it was just a few hundred feet away from the lake. "We should move the campers inland," we decided. Maybe we could redeem this camping trip after all. The guys were still gone by the time the kids were tired of the playground. Brandon and I teetered over the limestone boulders down to the lakeside so the kids could throw in sticks.

"Watch where you step. Don't get too close to the water." Our song sounded like a round between us, taking turns shouting at our kids. I had forgotten about the boulders along the lake, the ever-present danger we so readily ignored as kids ourselves, Bill, Phil, and me bold and leaping rock to rock. Poor Mom. Elvis and Lydia hunted for pebbles and sticks to throw into the water, their bodies wavering and swaying unbalanced by the shore. "Don't poke that stick in that hole; there might be a snake down there!" Brandon and I sat poised on our own rocks, shivering, prepared to catch one of our brave children if one tripped, certain it would happen any second. We couldn't take any more. "Okay, enough, let's go back to the campsite. Maybe Pop-Pop is back."

At lunch we moved the campers to a less windy part of the park. Phillip didn't come with my brother and dad, after all. His absence whistled through the branches overhead. Dad uttered his regret about their fight, "Phil should be here," he said as we walked toward the playground where the kids were playing with Brandon. Dad utters regret often these days. The *should've*'s and *could've*'s and *if only*'s roll out like waves in the wake of a speedboat on the lake. I try to soothe the burn when I can, shore up the tide with some *Look at all you've done for us* and *Look at all you've built around you* and *Look at your grandchildren, your children, your wife*, but it's only half-hearted—he *was* gone a lot. He worked hard, long hours. He came home worn out and weary. He didn't have time for play, or games, or vacation, just work and TV and sleep, precious sleep, napping on the couch, cap tipped low over closed eyes and snores, boots crossed at the ankles on the coffee table.

"He'll get over it," I said to Dad, about Phil, "You guys will work it out."

Bill and his wife walked down to the edge of the small inlet with Brandon, me, and the kids while Henry took his nap. The trees blocked the wind and permitted rays of light to dance on low waves. We showed the kids how to skip rocks across the shallow pond. It was just like old times, only instead of Dad or Grandpa, *we* baited the hooks, untangled the fishing wire, demonstrated how to cast and reel and then handed over the rod to eager fingers. When Lydia caught a fish, though, we asked Uncle Bill to let it loose, all of us squealing like a bunch of little girls as it bent against his palm.

In the months and years after Lydia reeled in her first fish (just a little four-inch bluegill), she will remind us of this moment, "Remember the time I caught a fish?" and I will hear myself at eight and nine and ten and eleven, reminiscing about the eight fish I caught with Dad on my eighth birthday. What a day that was, there by the shore of some anonymous pond in Geauga County, just me and Dad and a tackle box, a Styrofoam container of night crawlers in black soil, and two rods, just us, fishing silent alone together until we caught one, then two, then three, then four, then five, then six, then seven, then eight! Eight fish!

It was the same pond the five of us floated on in a rowboat sometime that same era of my childhood, maybe even that same summer. I can imagine myself begging to go back to the pond after we caught all of those fish; I can imagine bringing it up again and again to Dad. When, when can we go to the pond again, Dad? I'm sure it was just a shallow pool of water but it felt like it spread for miles. The top of the rowboat barely stayed above the surface as we paddled along, the five of us, all of us, Dad and Mom and me and Bill and Phil, together, rowing in a scary wooden boat around a pond. We got yelled at for almost tipping the boat, *hold still, sit in the middle, don't lean over the edge like that!* but the sun glistened on the surface, the cattails danced, frogs jumped into the water, and our hearts leapt with fear and joy. *Do you remember the fish? Do you remember the pond? Do you remember?*

After we all grew tired of casting and reeling, untangling fishing wire and re-baiting hooks, catching children before they were whacked in the eye by a mid-cast fishing rod, my husband played catch with Lydia and Elvis, and I chased Henry across the grass. And after the kids fell asleep that night,

Brandon poured me a glass of American Honey. We unfolded our "love seat" lawn chair, a navy blue two-seater, and sat around the campfire drinking and talking with my parents and Bill, keeping an ear turned toward our camper in case anyone stirred. Brandon brought out his guitar and started strumming. We had another round and stood while Brandon played John Mellencamp songs. Mom and I danced and sang along to "Jack and Diane" without a care about being out of tune, we laughed and swayed, "I love this song!" and "This is so great!" raising our hands and faces to the cloud-covered sky, all of us singing and drinking and warming ourselves by the fire, and me, grinning like I just caught my first sunfish by the water.

Camp Sandusky

I tossed my phone in the console cup holder, the battery at 10 percent after all of my attempts to refresh and find service, radar, weather alerts, Facebook updates, searching for signs of hope composed of no orange, yellow, and green splotches splattered on maps. I sighed.

"Okay, here's what I think we do," Brandon said. "There's a McDonald's on the other side of the highway, and they usually have free Wi-Fi. Let's go and grab a snack—ice cream, kids?—"

"Yeah!"

"—and see what happens," for this last part, our eyes met, doubtful about the storm clouds in the distance, the missing rays of sun.

As the kids licked their ice cream cones and climbed around and over the sticky yellow and red plastic chairs, the torrent calmed to a gentle drizzle that gave way to the occasional ripple on a dip in an asphalt puddle and then only clouds heavy with the threat of rain, no more lightning, the potential for rain gray but, yes, I think it's lightening, brightening a bit, don't you think?

We checked in to Camp Sandusky and rolled down the mud and limestone drive of the campground.

"Look! There's the pool! And there's the playground! It looks like a castle!" the kids said, clawing at the windows, pointing at the slouching slides, rusting chain-link ladder, the rotting boards and chipping paint, the faded Little Tikes play sets. All I saw were puddles and mud, puddles and mud. Brandon chuckled under his breath, snickering as I slouched and sighed in the passenger seat. The campground was deserted except for a car or two and a thirty-foot motorhome. We pulled to a stop in front of our very own ten-by-ten shed.

"Wow! I can't believe we get to stay in a *real cabin!*" Lydia said, springing from the back seat and sprinting to the small deck the size of a wood pallet. The cabin had two electric outlets and a bare bulb light fixture attached to the wall, a set of bunk beds, a thin double mattress on a wood frame, and enough space for Henry's pack 'n' play, a floor fan, and our duffle bags of clothes. Behind the cabin, semis and cars and trucks and trailers roared, muted by a small stand of wild grasses and sumac.

"I get the top bunk!" Lydia announced and proceeded to roll out her Disney Princess sleeping bag while Elvis spread out his Pixar Cars sleeping bag. Henry crawled around on our bed giggling and fleeing from me. Brandon grabbed his hammer and started pounding at the nails that protruded from our porch.

We spent the afternoon in the pool, Lydia rejoicing that she was tall enough to touch in the shallow end while Elvis clung to me as one tense muscle—a comic bundle of nerves giggling and shrieking in terror, and Henry, just turned two, attempting with every ounce of energy in him to detach from his parents' grasp and swim away. Except he couldn't swim. None of them could swim, not yet, not with any confidence or control, not without inadequate, frantic kicks and gulps of chlorinated water, gagging.

After Brandon and I couldn't handle anymore "swimming," we wandered back to the cabin, chasing Henry away from mud puddles. Dinnertime was approaching. The natives grew restless. They played UNO while we unloaded the firewood and unpacked food. I worried a little about starting a fire—I mean, I *know* how to start a fire and all, but this was traditionally my dad's role. With some fancy footwork and balancing skills, I leaned each piece of wood in a pyramid and jammed a few wads of paper underneath, and it crackled to life. We pulled our patio chairs around the fire and cooked Italian sausages.

"Don't get too close!" we scolded. After dinner, we roasted the obligatory marshmallows, some burnt and charred, some toasted golden, then sat entranced and watched the fire, reading Shel Silverstein poems, like "Ickle Me, Pickle Me, Tickle Me Too," before we escorted them off to bed, where they snuggled and giggled.

And then, finally, all was quiet in the cabin/shed ten feet away from our picnic table. The children slept. *What now,* I thought to myself, antsy for something to do, something to fill the space. All of those weekend camping trips of my youth ended with us kids in bed, our parents still sitting around the campfire. What did they talk about? What did they do in those quiet moments, after Mom cleaned up the pans and paper plates from dinner, after Dad worked in the summer heat on an excavator all day and then plowed and seeded the family corn fields in the evening, finally rolling into the campground as the sun began to set? All this time I had focused on what it meant to camp with my kids, and then it was just us. Just us.

It seemed as if Brandon and I hadn't had this much time alone in months, which was mostly true—our lives had been chaotic, his travel for work much more than anticipated. But that season was finally over, and it was summer, a brief respite before the fall football season began again. Brandon and I broke out the Firefly Sweet Tea Vodka and some ice and sat down across from each other at the picnic table.

"Want to play cards?" I asked.

"Sure, what do you want to play?"

"Let's play rummy." I shuffled the deck a few times and dealt. "This stuff is trouble," I said, sipping the tea. "It tastes just like sweet tea, not at all like alcohol."

I turned on my phone and played some music over Pandora. Johnny Cash and June Carter Cash sang "Jackson" then John Hiatt chimed in with "Feels Like Rain," and then Blake Shelton sang, "Honey Bee," and we sang along to the songs we loved, songs that have played into our story for the last decade.

"I play a lotta cards, obviously," I said, quoting *That Thing You Do.* "You gotta be quick with me; I'm from Erie, P-A." We played a lotta cards and poured some more, played some more cards and drank and drank. Brandon grabbed a bag of Tostitos and a jar of salsa to snack on, and we ate through the bag. We played to five hundred. I scored the highest round we'd ever seen in rummy but after a few hands, Brandon caught me and then won. When it got too dark to see the cards without squinting, we stacked the deck and crept over to the fire pit, its blaze dwindling since we roasted marshmallows with the kids a couple hours earlier. I put the last of our firewood into the ring and snuggled in next to my husband on our love seat—that double foldout chair we had traveled with to backyard barbecues and baseball games for the last decade.

In the time we'd had the chair it was rare for us both to settle in it together. We sat in it together to watch fireworks in our friends' backyard each Fourth of July. We sat in it together briefly at family picnics balancing plates of Barberton fried chicken and coleslaw on our laps, taking turns chasing toddlers around the yard or waiting for the other to respond to the bickering of our children. We sat in it last summer around the campfire with my parents. Mostly though, I brought it with me to watch him play double headers on Sundays in Akron, to afternoon ballgames he coached in Hartville while Lydia practiced taking her first steps between the families around the diamond, to Saturday morning soccer games optimistic the boys would let me sit, and to the t-ball field in Ashland as he helped to coach Lydia's first team while Elvis climbed trees and Henry picked blades of grass. It has lasted a good long while now, the fabric still firm, the metal still sturdy, if rusting a little in places. After a long fall, winter, and spring of sitting in the chair alone, it felt good to fold into Brandon's side. I sighed a contented sigh.

We watched the flames leap at the new wood and slowly burn down to red coals. The families and kids who had been at the amusement park all day drove up in a tour bus, a motorhome, a rusting SUV, and a parent's Mercedes. I refilled my glass another countless time and stumbled back to Brandon. By then the bottle was empty. "Oh, would ya look at that?" I pouted and staggered.

The minutes of the night flitted by like fireflies; we reflected on the spring and dreamt about the future, confessed career goals and fears. *Will this season ever end? Will we always be this busy? Is this what we will do forever?* We never imagined being here, never imagined this life. We cycle through these narratives every six months or so, in the quiet and undistracted minutes alone. Our marriage is not just tag-team grocery shopping and babysitting, laundry washed and folded, dinners discussed and cooked and eaten; no, we are creators and dreamers, lovers and friends, ambitious and insecure, weathering the seasons together as best as we can.

The travel made me nervous, the nights alone, our children's childhoods passing in a flash. I loved this life with him, this life we'd built together. I didn't want either of us to miss it, to whisper our regrets in decades down the road. I wanted more than regret, more than solitary fishing memories, more than quiet nights around a fire sipping vodka, then slipping off to sleep, longing to be filled.

The embers glowed orange, the fire crackled and popped, and in the silence I turned my face toward Brandon. We kissed, hard, the sweet tea vodka potent. No sounds from our sleeping children drifted from the cabin/shed. I lifted off my side of the chair and sat across Brandon's lap, engrossed and still passionately in love with this man, if not also a smidgen intoxicated, and we ran our hands through each other's hair and over each other's bodies. The family in the cabin a couple spaces down from us was forgotten, the kid who had asked to borrow a lighter for his fire was blaring some bad pop music hidden behind his parents' car, the high school kids on a youth group trip were nestled in their cabins far away from us. Brandon lifted my shirt over my head, and somewhere in those moments we made a collective decision to move away from the fire, off of the chair so awkward with him pinned underneath me, my lower legs numb from sitting on him. We stumbled behind the cabin, grateful for the steady roar of semis behind us, the electric fan whirring on the other side of the cabin's wall, the darkness to disguise the fun we had in the grass, fully absorbed in each other and lost in the delight of the night.

Afterward, I don't remember slipping into the cabin with him or putting anything away on the picnic table, just waking up at three a.m. cold and naked. I thought the cabin would be stifling all night but the evening breeze had cooled the room. I pulled in close to Brandon underneath the one lousy sheet I brought for us and tried to generate warmth.

We don't snuggle. After making love at home we're happy to roll to our respective corners of the bed and turn off the light, sigh, "That was awesome," and say good night, the Great Wall of China that is his body pillow wedged between us. But on that thin mattress with the cool night breeze blowing in through the windows and no clothes, we intertwined our limbs and hugged each other close, laughing and shivering and sleeping and waking. Around four in the morning, I broke down and snuck out the door to find a shirt and the Cleveland Indians throw blanket I'd used as a picnic tablecloth earlier. It was damp with dew. *Screw it*, I thought, quickly emptying the cards and cups onto the bench and lifting the wet blanket off of the table. At least it would keep our body heat in.

"Grab my jeans," Brandon whispered, and I brought them in, too. With the weight of the blanket on us, we shivered and snickered.

"If the kids wake up before six, let's get out of here," Brandon said under the whir of the fan, "Screw the pancake breakfast. We'll go to Panera."

"Amen." We curled into each other and slept lightly until 5:45 in the morning.

"Mommy? Daddy?" Henry said from his pack 'n' play in the corner. We brought him into our bed for a few more minutes until the older two awakened. They were only a little disappointed when we told them of our plans to pack up. Their enthusiasm spiked at promises of cinnamon crunch bagels and a stop at the McDonalds with the indoor playground.

"Did you guys have fun?" we asked. "What was your favorite part of the trip?"

"Sleeping in a *real cabin!*—Feeding the bison!—Swimming in the pool!—Playing catch with the football!—Roasting marshmallows by the fire!" The kids took turns shouting over each other and then quieted down again, looking out the window at the indoor waterparks and restaurants bordering the road.

"That was a lot of fun," Brandon said, glancing my way and then back toward the highway. "It's always good, but it isn't always fun. That," he said, "that was fun." I grinned and turned to face the road ahead. Yes, both good *and* fun. Good times. Fun times.

Friends in Low Places

WE WALKED DOWN THE sidewalk along the Daytona Beach drive in the dark, just Dad and me, my quick, bobbing, twelve-year-old step like skiing, attempting to match his long, unhurried stroll. I looked up at him. I grinned and lengthened my stride. *Step on a crack and you'll break your mother's back!* I chanted softly in my head. He dug a Zippo out of his back pocket, flicked the lid, spun the spark wheel against the flint and lit up his Winston cigarette. The tip burned orange, the only light between streetlights and zooming headlights as we walked.

In the bar down the road, we took turns around a game of eight-ball. I pushed the quarters into the slots and the balls cascaded out of their holding bin.

"Rack 'em up," he said, taking a swig of his Miller Lite. I rolled the balls across the felt, pushed them forward so they were tight against each other, then carefully lifted the rack away from the formation. "You want to break 'em?" he asked. I placed the cue ball in position.

This is what my father did as a young man in his early twenties with his dad, following a circuit of bars and pool tournaments to stay out of trouble, shooting pool and tipping back beers after abandoning his drug-addicted friends. That was before the late October afternoon in 1980 my grandfather yelled up to the roof where my dad was working, "Roger! Take Rosie to the concert!" my mom, the recently graduated girl next door, blushing madly and looking for my aunt who had planned to attend the Michael Stanley Band concert that night, before they married the next December, before I entered the picture as their blue-eyed girl born in late-July of '82. Dad taught me this game in the back of Auburn Inn underneath the low-hanging fluorescent light, next to the glowing jukebox I rushed to with quarters to play "There's a Tear in My Beer." Playing pool is a kind of family tradition.

I called stripes and he called solids. We surveyed the table for the best angles. I rubbed the tip of my cue stick with chalk and leaned forward, practicing the smooth pull back and let go between my index and middle finger, thumb resting on the rail, practiced back once, twice, then thrust, cracking the stick against the cue ball. It spun and ricocheted against the balls and then it was his turn to analyze and measure the distance between cue ball and the fifteen others around the table.

In between turns we took swigs from our drinks—his Miller Lite, my Pepsi with crushed ice. A karaoke DJ set up his speakers at the front end of the bar, away from the pool tables. When we finished our round, I grabbed a black binder of songs to see if we could find one to sing together. Back home, we sang along to the country radio, listened and jumped in when Grandpa and Grandma Fugman's bluegrass group strummed and played "Froggy Went a Courtin'." We sat across from each other at the wobbly orange table and read through the artists and song titles. There weren't many in the bar, maybe half a dozen others who watched the father-daughter out-of-towners troll through the songbook.

"How about 'There's a Tear in My Beer?'" I suggested, "or maybe a duet?" I listed off a hundred other songs and wiggled against the red plastic vinyl chair.

"Nah," Dad said, groaning, "Let me see this book." He turned the binder toward him, "How about Garth Brooks? 'Friends in Low Places?'"

A night like this could go one of two ways: Dad could latch on to the spirit and run, jubilant and drunk; or, Dad could slip south against the spirit and land, brooding and drunk. Not drunk, like falling over or unsteady, no, not my father, never out of control, never not contained, always under pressure like the cans of Miller Lite he sends me to fetch at home. Not drunk, like violent. Not drunk, like swerving. Drunk, like he's had a six pack or more, that's all, just a lot of alcohol, enough to loosen all the bound places. Maybe he burps and laughs and rubs his belly. Maybe he grimaces and grabs his chest with heartburn and asks for a couple Tums. Maybe he starts handing out hugs and "I love you's," eyes moist. Maybe he gets the regrets. Drunk, like human.

"So what do you think? 'Friends in Low Places?' A little Garth Brooks?" I agreed. I couldn't find a country duet that seemed like a good fit. The DJ called us up, handing each of us a microphone. I was nervous. So was Dad. The blue screen lit up with its white letters counting down in yellow four-three-two . . .

Dad came in early. I tried to sing over him, exaggerating a country drawl on "all" and the "oooh" of boots, turning red as we each belted out our version of the first verse off-key and out-of-sync, finally coming together for the chorus, the five or six in the audience embarrassed for us, my cheeks burning in shame at my own flat vocals paired with my dad's enthusiastic early entrance. It was as if we were two different people. We finished the song, handed the microphones back to the DJ, and slinked off the stage.

"Well, *that* was fun," Dad said, rolling his eyes and laughing, finishing off his Miller, then jerking his thumb over his shoulder. "Let's go!"

I took a final slurp of my pop and stood up to walk back to the beach house, the air heavy with ocean humidity, salt sticking to my skin, still trying to match my stride to his.

I Take to Drinking

IT'S JUST ONE GLASS to relax. My kids aren't asleep yet; I can hear Henry talking to his teddy bears in his crib, and Lydia and Elvis are still telling each other stories upstairs, giggling now and then, but otherwise the house is quiet. The television is off. I collect a few dishes from the dining room table and head into the kitchen to unload and reload the dishwasher, but before I start, I open the highest corner cabinet and consider my options: American Honey, Bailey's Irish Cream and Amaretto, Maker's Mark, or a glass or two of merlot.

This is what I do now, but I used to hate alcohol, all kinds. I shook the cans Dad sent me to fetch to make them flat, Miller Lite cans he drank from then stepped on with the heel of his work boot, cans crunched and piled in a dumpster behind his shop after hours, into the evening, and on the weekends. Those nights when he finally came back to the house, Dad wrapped his strong arms around me and smiled.

"I love you, Sare," he said. I rolled my eyes.

"I love you, too," I crooned. "Goodnight, Dad."

And there was the drink that kept my grandma away on holidays (not feeling well), the drink that made the dad of the kids I babysat for pass out on the floor before driving me home down dirt back roads, the rum my mom said made her sob so she wouldn't drink it anymore, but it was all kinds, especially beer, that goat piss yellow.

I sneered and turned up my nose at my peers, the high school boys and girls who gathered around campfires at their parents' houses on weekends underage drinking and drinking and drinking. Here I am, now, sipping a generous pour of American Honey from a glass tumbler, sighing, alcohol warm down my throat.

❄

I took to drinking malt beverages first because they tasted like liquid candy instead of the sour water of Millers, "fruit-flavored" wine coolers I could twist the bottle cap off and take a swig without a grimace. It started when I studied abroad in Australia for a semester my freshman year of college, where it was okay to drink at eighteen. I followed the rules. I obeyed the law. The Americans joined the Aussies in the merry, slightly startled looking party. Aussies know how to hold their alcohol. I hula hooped for a lemon Stolychnaya Ruski; it was paradise hot, the bar was open air, everyone sat at picnic tables, clapping, cheering, counting to ten as I hula hula hula won! This was the first drink I actually *liked*. I drank it down as if it was fair lemonade, pressed the rim of the glass against my lips.

Eric squeezed my waist, so proud of his girl and her hula, her smile, her empty bottle. Later, I lectured him about drinking.

"It's just that, you're different when you drink," I said, the "I love you's" quicker, easier, just like my dad, just like him.

"I'm not like your dad," he said and laughed, tipping back an amber bottle.

I hated alcohol. I hated the way it burned a hole through the casing around a man's emotions so they could leak out uninhibited. I hated the way the hangover sealed tight whatever cracked the night before and coated it in bitters.

Back home, Dad drank a six pack a day, at least.

I drank just one. I was careful.

But this *new* boyfriend, this *new* man knew these things about me and didn't care whether I drank. By then, I didn't care—as much—either. My fiancé drank a beer on occasion, a bottle once in a while at a backyard party, something accompanying dinner. I slurped a strawberry daiquiri with my parents and brothers and husband-to-be at Pickle Bill's for my twenty-first birthday, where I snapped through and pulled out the meat from all-you-can-eat crab legs.

Wait, did I even order an alcoholic beverage? Or was I still above a buzz, afraid to be under the influence, insistent I could have a fine time completely sober? And I could, absolutely I could, order whatever you want, I'll have a Pepsi instead.

"What do you mean, you are thinking about a dry wedding?" Dad said, voice rising in volume. Brandon worked at a Christian school and we weren't sure how it might be perceived if alcohol was served at our wedding. We were concerned about appearances. "We are not inviting all of our friends to a wedding that isn't going to serve alcohol. What kind of a party is that?" Dad said, red-faced, and I was quick to back down, okay, beer and wine but no liquor.

Wine is fine but liquor is quicker, I thought to myself, but it doesn't matter; this was a Miller and Bud drinking crowd, not martinis or amaretto sours or straight up Jameson drinkers, like we will be, later.

"Do not get drunk on wine, which leads to debauchery. Instead, be filled with the Spirit, speaking to one another with psalms, hymns, and songs from the Spirit," I read, my NIV Study Bible weathered, its spine broken and pages noted, Ephesians verses underlined, "Sing and make music from your heart to the Lord, always giving thanks to God the Father for everything, in the name of our Lord Jesus Christ."

Amen. It's the Spirit alone I consumed, the Spirit that moved. But Brandon would drink, and when we went out to line dance, the bottles lined the bar. I gulped from a plastic cup of water, then surged back to the polished floor for another cha-cha and watched as my husband loosened up, and suddenly he wanted me, he was singing too loudly in my ear and swinging me tight around the dance floor.

Other nights, we met our friends at Boccasio's, a bar we didn't think any of the other believers would be and ordered our drinks in secret. It was karaoke night and Brandon belted out bar favorites—"You Never Even Call Me By My Name" by David Allan Coe, "The Fireman" by George Strait, "Live Like You Were Dying" by Tim McGraw, or maybe some Rolling Stones, Beatles, Elvis tunes, anything to get a rise from the crowd. I tried on Sara Evans's "Suds in the Bucket," which wasn't quite a "Tear in My Beer" but it was close. I was still sober, sober and insecure, but I sang the lyrics anyway.

I wrinkled my nose at all of the bottles, "Gross," I said, "I don't know how you drink this stuff."

Instead, I tried white wines and sangrias. I tried margaritas. I tried daiquiris and sours and Long Island iced teas. I tried red wines, eventually, after the burnt oak flavor wore away and I had "acquired a taste" for this water-to-wine beverage, this merlot and sauvignon and shiraz, words I practiced pronouncing for the feel of them in my mouth, their tannins, their full-bodied flavor. I tried these drinks with friends whose palates were more sophisticated than mine. We drank one, or two, maybe three, and then I was laughing and speaking as one with authority, wit quick and sharp if just a little slurred. *So this is why people drink*, I thought.

I wondered how much is too much, whether drinking could be done with any control. Could it be simply enjoyed, with a little moderation? Was it ever okay to drink? Was it never okay to drink? Was it always okay to drink? My husband came home around one or two in the morning from singing at another karaoke night with friends. It was dark. I was startled. He shook me awake, *I couldn't say no, I don't know how to stop*, and I held him, and we stopped, for a while, we didn't drink, for a while. He remembered his alcoholic grandfather; I remembered my mom's Al-Anon book. It was whispering around the edges of our conversations—can we hold our alcohol, can we say no, do we know how to stop, are we dependent, alcoholism coursing through our genetic code?

After we left the Christian school bubble and arrived in a more moderate work world, after our crisis of church and hunt for an authentic community of believers—we wanted to be people who were unafraid to drink with other people who were unafraid to drink—Brandon and I sat at the bar in a New York City hotel and ate and drank. It was a writer's conference for work, and we were there, together, alone. The waitress brought me my sour apple martini. I sipped it and ate and we laughed and felt shell-shocked but free, free, *free* of the two children under two that were back at home with our parents. My glass was empty and then we ordered another round that came late.

"I'm so sorry, I forgot!" the waitress said. "I'll bring you another round." We looked at each other and laughed—we were still in debt, the drinks were on the house—and drank it up.

Three martinis later, "I'm going to need your help," I giggled, drunk, for the first time *so* drunk, stupid drunk, lobby of the hotel spinning drunk, and Brandon propped me up tight against the earthquake. He negotiated the distance between our booth and the elevator, then pressed the button, and I leaned, heavy against him, leaned, all the way to our room, and all I wanted was him. Immediately.

I nibbled his ear. We shivered out of our clothes and into the bed with a splash of sheets and blankets rippling, rolling like waves in that king-size bed. The room spun and spun and spun and still nothing, still nothing, *okay, okay,* I thought, *I'm tired now, enough,* all I wanted was to sleep, so tired, so hot, so drunk, so drunk.

"Go, eat your food with gladness, and drink wine with a joyful heart," I read in my Bible again, this time from Ecclesiastes, "for God has already approved of what you do." I am still a good girl. I still obey the rules. We meet friends at a wine bar thirty minutes away and split a flight of wine—a flight, the way spirits rise and take wing, so free—and then split another flight again. We drink and drink, laugh and laugh and drink, eat a couple of flatbread pizzas and read the wine descriptions. *Can you taste the tannins?* We laugh. *This is such a robust wine!* We snicker, *What is a tannin?* We look it up on our phones, *Google that shit!* we shout and laugh but don't remember the definition later. Somehow, we all drive home. Somehow, we are not arrested. Somehow, I make it up the stairs, crawl up the stairs, one knee and hand in front of the other, laughing, laughing, woozy, spinning.

"Just look at you, you're no good to me now," Brandon laughs out a line from *That Thing You Do.* I groan and smile, crawling into my side of the bed.

That night at the West Branch campground while the fire crackled and our three children slept and we gathered with my parents around the campfire, Brandon brought me a drink.

"I think you'll really like this," he said. I took a sip. It was sweet and warm going down, and strong.

"Mmm, that's nice," I said, "What is it?"

"American Honey."

"Mmm," I said, sipping again. Soon, I was standing and singing at the top of my lungs with my mom and dad while my husband strummed the guitar, singing to the night, singing to the sky, singing because we love to sing, we love this song, "*This is the best song ever!*" we yelled and sang. We were so happy, so in love, so funny, so free, the fire dying, our glasses filled and refilled.

We came to bourbon and whiskey together even though his friends introduced them—Jack's okay but Maker's is better, Jameson, Jefferson's Reserve, Basil Hayden's, Elijah Craig, or Woodford Reserve all acceptable, desirable. He orders a double pour, neat. I like the heat on the back of my throat, the warm glow, tension loosened and then shed on the floor. I make a hot toddy when my throat's feeling sore—hot water over a shot of whiskey and a spoon of raw honey and suddenly my spirit is quiet. I smile over the edge of my mug and snuggle under the covers. We clink our glasses and sip. "Cheers!"

It is warm here.

Brandon is on the road again. This is my evening routine lately, I kiss the kids goodnight, gather up the cookware and silverware from dinner, unload the dishwasher, reload the dishwasher, wipe down the counters, and turn off the kitchen light. I have a seat on the couch in the living room and pop open my laptop or crack the spine of a book or flick through the movies I've DVRed, and write or read or watch TV, or all of those at once. And drink.

The Face of Mercy

Dorm Rooms

I MET LISA THE summer before fifth grade at the end of a fishing dock during a camping trip at Pymatuning State Park. Our more extroverted brothers had found each other, and our moms had encouraged us introverts to meet, as well, to see if we liked the same books or something. We've been friends, on and off, ever since. She's the sort of friend you just can't seem to shake. Despite our best efforts to break our relationship, God has kept drawing us together, even after we had exchanged hateful letters in seventh grade, even after high school graduation, our college selections the same, our dorm room assignments the same.

So there we were, comfortably stuck together in Amstutz Hall Room 813. In a late night crisis moment, I had begged Jesus to save me and help me with my life the fall of my freshman year, and suddenly, the floodgates of Scripture poured over me. I sopped up verses like a sponge.

"Listen to this!" I squealed from my lofted single bed, underlining and highlighting and rewriting verse after verse after verse. I had cried over Eric again and again and read to her Bible verses like she had never heard them before, only she had, forever. Jesus and church were what her family did. In middle school, she had tattooed in ink a pile of initials of people she was praying would come to know Jesus. Mine were always among them. Now, I knew Jesus. The Bible that had seemed so foreign and strange was suddenly opening itself up to me.

"Have you ever heard anything so beautiful?" I asked, quoting and underlining some more.

"Mmm hmm," she muttered, turning back to whatever she was working on at two in the morning. That fall, we prayed together through difficult classes and suffered through the flu with boxes of Kleenexes. She confessed her secrets to me and I cried. I confessed my worries to her and she held me.

In the spring of my freshman year, I followed Eric to Australia for a semester. Lisa mailed me a packet of cards and a list of verses, "For when you are lonely. For when you are afraid. For when you feel unworthy." I looked them all up and underlined them in my NIV Study Bible. I often felt alone and afraid and unworthy that spring, so far away, trying to discern what the future should hold for me, with or without Eric, in this degree program or that, at this school or that, with this God or that. I missed my best friend. Communication was hard from the other side of the ocean. She had a boyfriend now, too. In desperation one night, I called her from a laundromat in New Zealand in the midst of a crisis with Eric.

"What should I do?" I asked her.

"You should break up with him," she said.

"I know. But we're in another country together," I argued.

"That's true," she said.

I didn't break up with him, of course. We'd take breaks on and off for another year and be friends (with benefits) until the following spring.

The semester in Australia ended, and Lisa and I decided to buy-out singles, to live our lives a little more separately on the same campus. Those separate lives conjured separate challenges, and distance. When Lisa and her boyfriend of several months broke up, it caused a weirdness with our group of friends. We stopped eating the same meals together. We didn't always walk to class at the same time.

Deep in the heart of the fall semester of our sophomore year, Lisa asked me to come over to her dorm room, the same one we had shared the previous fall. She wanted to discuss something. Her tone was cold and controlled.

He violated me, she said. I blinked.

"What do you mean?" I asked. "What happened?"

His dorm room door was closed, she said, and they never kept it shut. Things happened. She didn't want them to happen. She hovered above her body and watched what was happening to it, frozen. I shook my head, no. No. I knew her now ex-boyfriend. I knew this religion major, this aspiring pastor, this mutual friend. I had coached him on giving her space, on letting her go. The breakup had been hard on him, and I had been there, sorry for him and hopeful they could make it work. I didn't like to see things end.

"Are you sure?" I asked, "Are you sure?" meaning *Are you sure you didn't want it? Are you sure that's what he meant?*

I've done far more with boys, far more has been done to me by boys. I didn't know how boys thought, but now I knew what they did. In the movie theatre in eighth grade, Kevin's sloppy tongue and groping hands reached to touch what wasn't ready to be touched. Chris in the park pavilion my sophomore year of high school unlatched his belt, my undressed skin sharp against the picnic bench, the *no* I whispered apologetically, shamefully, too young to feel anything else except embarrassment. There I was, too, learning what boys did, the empty girl in Los Angeles when Eric was gone, longing for anyone to love me, anyone to fill me with something. There I was, sandwiched between the mattress and a college guy whose name I don't remember, letting him undress me in his hotel room. "Don't worry, I never go all the way the first night," he had said. I just nodded and watched what was happening to my body there on the bed, spirit hovering in the corner.

Some things had been done to me by boys. This is how boys are.

"It must have been a misunderstanding," I said, uncomfortable, searching her face, so cold, so controlled.

"This friendship is over," she said. I didn't know what to say.

"Lisa—"

"No, just leave."

So I left.

I left her there.

Jesus.

Late Night Living Rooms, Part One

When I accepted my new job in Ashland, one of the first concerns I had was meeting Lisa somewhere, a chance run-in down the bread aisle, pumping gas, or walking to the rec center to exercise. It had been four years since we had last spoken. Ashland is too small to go too long without a happenstance passing.

So much had changed.

At night, I dreamt of Lisa. In my dreams she confessed to me that she planned to die, explained how she might commit suicide. I spent each variation of the nightmare attempting to rescue her, chasing her, hiding knives and broken glass and rope, stopping her from falling off of buildings. I woke up worried. Where was she? What was happening? A quick Facebook stalk confirmed her Ashland residence, married too, now, to a much older man with two kids from his first marriage. She should've been my maid of honor. I should've been hers.

I broke the silence on Facebook before we moved to Ashland in a message sent to give her the heads up, "Hey! Guess what weird thing is happening."

One evening months after we moved in, she came over with wine and cookies and a bag of monogrammed towels.

"Don't you remember?" Lisa said, "We joked about giving each other monogrammed towels with our new last initials for wedding presents. These are a little late, but no matter."

"Thanks," I said, forgetting and then remembering the inside joke along with dozens of others we held between us. We talked and talked, laughed and talked, husbands, children, wine, miscarriages, her recent marriage, step-children, travel. Then elephants. Giant room-sized elephants.

"I'm really sorry I didn't believe you," I said. "That I wasn't there to support you." Lisa blinked a few times. I didn't have to say what I meant; she knew exactly what I meant. We locked eyes, and I continued, "I was wrong. I should have believed you. I should have supported you and stood by you, and instead I left you." I didn't know I was going to say these words until they were out of my mouth, surprised by the sudden rush of confession. It was so quiet in my living room, nothing but the fan whirring, the occasional car passing outside. "I should have been a better friend. I need you to know I'm so sorry."

"Wow," Lisa said. "You don't know how much that means to me. I forgive you," she said, "and I know that I wasn't always the best friend for you, either. I'm sorry, too."

We each took a sip of wine, a bite of a cookie.

"You know," I said, "I used to have dreams about you."

"What?!"

"Seriously! I was always trying to rescue you."

"That's crazy. I dreamt about you, too. I was always trying to get away from you."

Late Night Living Rooms, Part Two

The night I realized sending over two hundred text messages to a new male friend might be bad for my marriage, I texted Lisa.

"Hey."

"Hey! How are you?"

"Not good."

"Want to come over?"

"Yes."

"See you in a minute."

"K."

"I'm going over to Lisa's for a little bit," I told Brandon on my way out our front door.

"Okay. Is everything okay?" he asked.

"Yup. I'll see you soon. Love you."

Lisa's house had a strange odor. Old books and mildew, sure, but something more, maybe old horsehair in plaster, something ancient, something pungent and unique to that space. It was embedded in the cookies she brought over that first night we spent hanging out together. Later, we'd wonder about that odor, how it lingered in car trunks and boxes. It was the smell of something gone wrong.

I let myself in. Her husband wasn't home. Neither were her step-kids, and we grabbed a glass of wine each and sat across from each other on her couch.

"What's up?" she asked.

I told her about the guy I had met the week before at the writer's residency. We had a lot in common—he was married with kids, a writer who cared a lot about faith and wrote about faith and there are so few of us and we talked for hours and laughed and cracked jokes by text message during evening readings and when he left we just kept texting because we make each other laugh and he's married with kids so is it a big deal? What's the big deal? Sure, it's a lot of text messages, but that's all. Just friends. Just friends.

And yet. The unease I felt had dragged me down the stairs of my house, passed my husband, out the front door, into my car, down the street, onto her couch. Just friends.

"Do you wish each other goodnight?" Lisa asked.

"We just said goodnight, tonight, to each other," I said. Just now. Just a minute ago. Just friends. A rocket of panic untethered in the pit of my stomach and launched itself through my chest, into my throat. "Right before I texted you."

"You have to end this now, Sarah," she said. "I know you don't want to, but you have to. And you have to tell Brandon."

"What!" I cried. That seemed a bit extreme, to me. Nothing had happened. Nothing! It's totally innocent, and besides, he lives out of state. He's so nice. He's so funny. He cares about my writing.

"You have to tell him. Whatever is drawing you to this guy is only a symptom of something else you aren't getting from your marriage."

I looked at her and away.

"If you don't tell him, how can he help you? How can he help protect your marriage?"

I nodded, face wet. *I'm crying. I can't believe I'm crying about this.*

I didn't want to stop talking to him. He was a genuinely good person, kind, in love with his wife and kids. *I* was in love with my husband and kids. *What's wrong with me,* I thought to myself, that I can't hold up some boundary, that this kindness was already creeping between me and my husband?

From outside my internal hurricane, Lisa continued.

"You know that we've had some problems," she said, looking off to a corner, "after the miscarriage. We were going for counseling. Well, there's more. I'm only here tonight to pack. I'm leaving Jeff. I had my own trouble, with a guy, only it wasn't this innocent. We didn't know what was happening, until it happened."

Lisa's words filtered through my own storm, registering slowly.

"That's not the only reason I'm leaving. Jeff is on vacation with his family. I was supposed to go to Italy, but I couldn't imagine that. I couldn't do it. I'm staying with a friend in Wooster. I'm leaving tonight."

"I'm so sorry. Wow. What timing."

"All I'm saying is you have to tell Brandon," Lisa said, "And you have to end this, now, tonight. Don't let it continue."

Bedrooms

"This is affecting my marriage," I wrote, the note apologetic for how I had escalated this friendship in my mind. It was hard to send that message. It felt silly to be so affected, so weak. He apologized and bowed out, and that was that. Just like that.

And then I told Brandon what had happened, curled against the bed in the night, shaking about how *nothing had happened, nothing had happened,* but how much I needed him to know that nothing had happened. Brandon was silent.

"Well, aren't you going to say something?" I whispered.

"What do you want me to say?" he said. "What do you want me to do? You want me to tell you I want to punch a hole in the wall? Because that's what I want to do."

I did, kind of, want him to say that, to do that. This mattered. I mattered. My heart beat hard in the silence of our bedroom. Brandon paced in the dark, then got into bed. I curled against his back, then turned away and wept. He curled against my back and wept. We turned toward each other and wept. It was a long night. And then we slept.

The First Step Is Admitting
You Have a Problem

"There is more to life than increasing its speed."

— *MAHATMA GANDHI*

Blog post, dated March 5, 2013

I LEAVE IN THE morning. I'm leaving with my homework done for this week, four manuscripts formatted and sent to print for work in February, a grant written and *almost* submitted, all of the laundry in the house done, dishes washed, fridge stocked, living room and dining room vacuumed and clean, and all of my children healthy. Elvis is home from Akron Children's Hospital after discovering a *freaking kidney stone* on Saturday. *A kidney stone.* In a *five year old.* Why, Universe, why?

I've also finished several glasses of wine.

My husband is supposed to fly in tonight from Baltimore to Cleveland, but it's delayed, hopefully not cancelled. I need to leave the house at five in the morning to go to Boston from Cleveland. If he's cancelled, which he might be, he's arranged for a friend to come over to be with the kids so I can leave. Which is helpful. At least there's a contingency plan.

My eye won't stop twitching. It's been doing it for weeks now, and it's really starting to drive me nuts. I feel a little bit like Meryl Streep in *It's Complicated*, holding my eye lid up with my finger all day.

I need this trip. I need this trip to try to regain some sanity, to try to slow down for just a second and not feel guilty for not doing something I should be doing. Like right now, I should be putting the clean clothes away. I should be sweeping the kitchen floor. I should be reading through the school newsletter so that I know what's going on with Lydia's class. I should know *something* about what's going on in my kids' school lives. I shouldn't be whining. I should just get over it, suck it up, like I've been doing, and stop making such a big deal out of it because it isn't a big deal, right, right?! *Right?!*

Only I'm so tired. I can't sleep, though, because if I sleep I'll dream about flies hatching from underneath my fingernails, like last night. If I sleep, I'll miss my alarm and miss my plane. If I try to go to sleep before I'm thoroughly worn out I will lie there and catalog whatever it is that is left to do on my to-do list that I'm ill prepared for or certain to forget about in the morning. Better to Google, "How to know when you're having a nervous breakdown." Better to watch *Harry Potter #3* and drink another glass of wine and eat another piece of dark chocolate.

I want to quit everything. I want to quit, to quit, to quit, burrow under my blankets and stay there until the Universe remembers that I am its center and it should do exactly as I tell it to, like we've discussed several times before, but noooooo, the Universe ignores me and does whatever the heck it wants.

I didn't work today because of the whole five-year-old-in-the-hospital-for-freaking-kidney-stones episode, which actually allowed me the space and time to reassemble the house that exploded on Saturday with unfolded/crumpled clothing and dirty dishes from the dinner I made but didn't eat because of the kidney-stone episode.

I know I'm not alone, but I feel so *alone*. I don't want to ask for help because I'm always asking for help, but if I don't ask for help my eye twitches more and my heart starts to race and my hands start to shake and I start bawling my eyes out like I'm doing right now sitting in my kitchen sobbing like a four-year-old that's denied his ice cream cone. I feel guilty for asking for help because I should be able to *do this*, it isn't that hard, what's so hard about working and taking care of your kids and doing a little reading and writing here and there? What's the big deal? Why can't I keep it together?

I don't know what to give up or let go in order to regain some semblance of sanity. And because I don't know what to give up, I want to quit it all, to say goodbye to work and to school, to retreat into my house and leave only to get my kids off to their respective schools, buy groceries, and go to yoga when I can because I need someone to remind me to breathe.

But, like I've said a thousand times before, I am not a four-year-old who has been denied an ice cream cone. I am a wife. I am a mother. I am a faithful employee. I believe in my work and my family and my marriage and my God and my writing, and I know what I do is good and right, and I need to keep doing it, even though right now I'd like to curl into the cave. This is what we do. We keep on going. It's only one really, really, really, long season. It has to end sometime.

So, *deep sigh* I will finish this, switch the last load of laundry, refill my wine glass, turn on something light and funny, or *Harry Potter #3*, and stop thinking for a while. Whatever I forgot to pack can be purchased in Boston. They actually have stores there, so no big thing. And, if I do miss my alarm and miss my flight, hey, guess what, they fly more than one airplane to Boston. Perhaps the hardest thing about this mini-mental-breakdown season of my life is that I know it isn't futile. I know there's hope and an answer to the busyness, and I know that part of my problem is pride—I am proud of keeping this life balanced precariously on the edge of sanity. Look at me, I'm doing it, I'm surviving! But I don't want to just survive. I want to thrive. To live a life of contentment, as recommended by the good ol' Solomon in Ecclesiastes.

Perhaps the only real crisis will be if I don't hurry up and refill this wine glass.

Tomorrow is a new day with its own worries, and thank God, thank *God, thank GOD* his mercies are new every morning. He is faithful, even if his faithfulness appears in my mind like Trace Adkins shaking his head and singing, "You're Gonna Miss This." I am grateful for the myriad ways he has been merciful. God, not Trace. Although maybe Trace Adkins is also merciful, I don't know.

Blog post, dated March 13, 2013

Who is that crazy person? Woah. She's crazy, isn't she?

She hasn't completely moved out, but I think I've at least stashed her polka dot and pinstripe clown suit in the closet for a couple of days.

Boston was restorative. I slept a lot, ate good food, and had great conversations with some amazing women and a few good men. I sold books and talked about writing and reading and slept. Sunday morning, I ordered breakfast in bed and wrote for three hours until it was time to check out and fly home. And then I played with my children and saw my husband who was not a mirage but the actual thing in flesh and blood not tucked in Skype or my phone but the real deal, and it was very good.

The crazy person in me still feels a little unstable, still cries easily and flinches when something unexpected happens. My eye still twitches. But we have a few strategies to manage her now, I think. Here are your instructions, Crazy:

#1: Take life cut into triangles drizzled with maple syrup. If you try to jam that big of a piece in your mouth like that it'll make you gag and that's just gross, so cut it into bite-size pieces, and make sure it's sweet. Get up fifteen minutes earlier, for God's sake, and slow the morning down a smidgen. Start the day with a Word so it sticks to your hips like the pancakes. Get everyone off to their respective destinations, and then breathe because you're at the day job and the day job has manageable to-do lists, meetings, phone calls, goals and instant gratification. The work day does what it's told and doesn't talk back because you're the boss (well, of your work day, anyway) and that's what work days do, they do what they're told, that's right, you know it. Then return everyone to their destinations of origin for food (home-cooked if you're able, and if not, don't beat yourself up, they won't die from that cheeseburger . . . at least not today), baths, and bed. Try to make bedtime stories and prayers and songs happen. Try. And then breathe again, take a few hours to drink a glass of wine, write, read, and listen to quiet music.

#2: Sneak in some exercise here and there because you know how good it feels to get a good sweat on. Even if it means skipping your lunch break to get to the gym, do it. Just do it. You can even drop the crew off at the childcare station after work, even though you feel guilty about all of this childcare but hey, better to have a sane mom some of the time than a crazy one all of the time.

#3: Be content with adequate for once. Be content because nobody is impressed with 150 percent . . . they think you're crazy *and you are*. Those looks are pity, not awe. Those looks are, dude, you're crazy.

#4: Cancel the spring soccer practices and games. No one is going to miss it, not even for a minute, and baseball is right around the corner, when your husband's crazy schedule loosens up, and you won't have to tote the gang into the rain on Saturday mornings alone. Lydia might be sad for about ten seconds and then she'll be over it and on to coloring and dancing and laughing and light.

#5: Don't substitute another weekly activity for the one you just cancelled, i.e., no swimming lessons, gymnastics practices, dance, ballet, tap, piano, karate, etc. you crazy person just let it go so you can enjoy your children for more than the minutes they are sleeping silently in their beds.

#6: The laundry can wait until Saturday.

#7: The dishes can wait until . . . there aren't any more clean ones.

#8: Don't shut down and shut out your friends and family, even though it's tempting to hole up, burrow in, and battle through alone, even though it feels safer and warmer under these covers. Coffee is good. Wine is better.

#9: Even though he's on the road and working, call and text your husband, who loves you and misses you, and believe it when he says it because it's true and you know it's true that this is just a season and crazy will end one day in the foggy not-so-distant future that feels a million years from here.

#10: Read instead of watch TV. Write instead of scroll through Facebook.

#10: Sleep, you dimwit. You need it. After all, you just made two #10s.

III.

The wife, where danger or dishonor lurks,
Safest and seemliest by her Husband stays,
Who guards her, or with her the worst endures.

— JOHN MILTON, *PARADISE LOST*, BOOK 9

Not-My-Husband

IN THE QUIET OF a summer night, crickets chirping and sun setting, sipping a glass of American Honey on the back patio with my husband, I text my colleague to see if he wants to swing by and pick me up to grab a drink.

"Sure, I'll be there in a few mins. Still at WalMart."

He is in town for a few weeks for a conference, and besides our regular emails and Facebook messages, it's been a while since we've had a face-to-face conversation. I'm eager to catch up in person, ready to talk about the rumors that his marriage might be falling apart. We have been friends for years now; we exchange witty back-and-forths and like each other's Facebook posts. *How are things at home?* I ask in a Google chat window, *Do your kids sense the tension?* I ask in a Facebook message. I want to encourage him to stick it out.

Brandon scrolls through his Twitter feed in the patio chair across from me until the night sky is dark, our glasses empty, and we wander back inside. When my colleague finally arrives, our other friend isn't with him, and a small ping of a warning bell dings inside my head. He comes in through the front door and shakes hands with Brandon. The three of us talk and joke in the dining room, where I have hung half a dozen photos of our wedding day and pictures of the kids, before we head toward the door.

"I'll be back soon," I say, hugging my husband, "I love you."

"Love you too, babe." And the door swings closed on its loud hinges, clasps shut, the front stoop light glowing orange in the night.

My friend and I drive to the dive-iest of dive bars in town to talk and drink. I order a whiskey, neat. He thinks it's crazy that I like whiskey. I drink it. I order another. All we do is talk and talk, talk and talk.

I don't feel as if I'm saying anything different than I normally would, but he says, "I'm seeing a whole other side of you, Swells," laughs, looks me in the eyes too long. Maybe it's because I'm looser with my opinions, freer with our usual wit and banter, the things I say about my job and my writing and my life a little bit funnier, a little bit sassier, and all of this taking place mostly in email, until now. I grin like a little kid and turn back to the bar.

In a candid email about work earlier that spring, I made a joke about why the school keeps me around, and my friend said, "Not just eye candy then?"

Eye candy? I had frowned. Oh. That's right. I am a female. He is a male. "Let's stick to the nickname 'Swells," I replied, but it had been so long since I had felt physically attractive, coming off eight years of being pregnant and then not being pregnant and then trying to be pregnant, over and over again. Now, Henry was nine months old. I ran a half marathon the previous fall with my mom, shedding baby weight and building muscle. Brandon and I changed our eating habits in the spring and I lost ten more pounds, just five away from what I weighed on my wedding day. People commented on how good I looked. *Eye candy?* Really? Later, he apologized for crossing the line, that invisible line between friendly chiding and flirtation, the small fissure in the wall patched for the time being.

But here in the bar, I don't really know what I'm doing, I'm not really sure where this is going, except that I *like* this guy, I've liked this guy for a long time, he's a great friend, so fun to talk to, so fun to be with. But *eye candy* buzzes and lands like a fly on my thigh. I spin back and forth on the barstool; I ask again about his marriage, his kids. What's happening? Why is it falling apart? "It's my fault," he says, "Yeah, the kids can tell. They sense the tension."

I order another drink and a large glass of water. Where is the line between friendly conversation and flirtation once you're married, once you are on a barstool next to a male friend? With several whiskeys behind me, I don't know when it crosses over. The talk simply blurs until suddenly it leaks out, he's crushed on me for years—"but I was *pregnant* at that conference!"—I protest, still smiling, grinning too broadly, surprised to be desired.

"'Just so you know, I'm married," Brandon said to me, flashing his ring, "That's the first thing I say to women when I'm on the road." We laughed. It would be so easy to slip off the ring he holds up for their inspection.

"The trouble is," I told him over dinner in Lost River, West Virginia, "I prefer to talk to men," and he said between bites, "I know exactly what you mean. I enjoy talking to women." We left the restaurant holding hands, turned on James Taylor, slipped into the bed at the B&B and kicked off the sheets, broad daylight flitting through the blinds.

We're just friends as long as I hold up my end, I tell myself, as long as I hold up the bar with my forearms, as long as I keep shooing his palm off of my thigh. "No!" I screech, grinning. I'm insistent. I can't believe that he is touching me, that he could be so bold as to touch me that way, me, married, me, children, me.

"You have to stop touching me," I tell him. I *love* my husband. As his confessions start to whir, I say again, "You forget that I am happy in my marriage," and again, "You know, you are married too, sir" (it is his left hand he keeps trying to place on my leg).

"Are you going to tell Brandon about this, the way you told him about the other guy?" he asks. I blush and immediately regret my stupid alcohol confessional moments earlier, my open mouth and rambling on about what happened last year at this time, how blindsided by affection I had been.

"There's nothing to tell Brandon because *nothing is happening!*" I tell him. Nothing is happening. How do you tell someone you aren't attracted to them? "So what's your wife up to tonight?" I ask. He rolls his eyes.

"*I* love my husband." If I emphasize a new word each time I say it, I think, maybe it will buzz into his ear canal and nest.

He rolls his eyes again and looks down at his phone, which lights up now and then. His face falls into a shadow as he replies and then turns back to me, neon bar lights shining.

Happily married. Three kids. Thirty years old. I pay bills. I have a garden. My name is on the primary health insurance card. I love my husband. What on God's green Earth am I doing out without my husband, wearing these tight blue jeans and low-cut blouse laughing too much, gripping the edge of the bar?

He wonders this, too. "I was a little surprised when Brandon answered the door," he says, and it never occurred to me it would be awkward, because we're just friends—because we're just friends, because we're just friends—it runs like a train through my head. "Why are you here with me?" he asks.

"Because I wanted to talk to you about your marriage, because we're friends, because I enjoy your company." Because we're just friends!

I spin my rings around my finger with my thumb, feel the friction of flesh against metal, the weight of diamonds in a little row. I watch the bands as I twist them around my finger. They are counterfeit and real; my discount engagement ring against a wedding band with five tiny diamonds I insisted on. Of course I love my husband. Of course I am happy. My marriage isn't perfect. Who is happy all of the time? Whose marriage isn't both specks of gold and chunks of pyrite, specks of pyrite and chunks of gold, purified and refined and melted and molded? The whiskey in me disrupts these weaknesses, these places of tenderness in my marriage, the path a slow spiral.

"It's just that Brandon is gone a lot" and "there are things he doesn't say, things he doesn't do, that I miss sometimes . . . " and then,

"Careful, Sarah," not-my-husband says, "You don't want to go there." I blink out of my reverie and surface again, no, of course, I love my husband. And we're just friends.

This can't be me sitting on the barstool next to not-my-husband. I am standing next to the barmaid watching myself now, the alcohol separating brain from body, spirits exorcising spirit, the way it does when I've had too much, when I've gone too far. I watch this giddy thing spin on her barstool and drink whiskey too quickly. I watch this broad man, older than her, broad chested, clean-cut, professional, stare too long into her eyes, his hand occasionally leaping beyond the boundary of their friendship and landing on her leg. He stands up to play some music. She follows him to the jukebox and remarks about the posters on the walls, NASCAR paraphernalia, and beer signs; all so much like the ones in the bar her dad took her to when she was young. She keeps her distance from him, just out of arm's reach, and he croons to a song. He isn't drunk. They are married. They aren't married. They come back to their barstools and sip more water, pick up their phones and stare at the bright screens for a few seconds before they walk out the door. She sways a little but maintains control. He follows her, watches her from behind, and then the bar's door closes.

With the rush of summer air my spirit catches up with my body just as the car remote lock clicks open.

Thank you for a fun night, yes, good night good night a hug *good night* and then out of the passenger door, eyes watching every step, every blade of grass to the concrete sidewalk and up into the porch light, door unlocked, house dark, wedding photo in shadow on the wall, turn and watch his headlights highlight the driveway, the tree, the street and then nothing. Nothing happened. Nothing happened. Nothing. Except laughing and drinking and hours talking. Alone. With not-my-husband.

How much power do I have over this situation, how much control? *Am I even attracted to this man?* I wonder. Of course not, because we're just friends. *Of course not!* I love *my husband.*

"You look nice," my husband says as I head toward the door in my favorite dress, the one I wore to dinner with him in Lost River, West Virginia, a quick peck on the lips and a smile.

I keep thinking about you in that dress, says the text from not-my-husband that flashes on my phone. Heat rises. I run the hem of it between my fingers, the dotted line that holds the dress together.

After he has gone away, out of town, I breathe relief. Done. Gone. Away. But then we text and send messages online. He says things that make me blush and I reply with neutral words, never a *yes,* never a *no,* just passive resistance, a *shhh* while I try to hide my phone and Facebook posts. I delete the thread when it's over. *But you're married! I'm happy!* I keep protesting. I carry my phone close, panic if I leave my laptop open on the dining room table. Brandon has to know; I'm distant, irritable, lost in my own thoughts.

I know what I'm supposed to do. I've been here before. Lisa's words rattle around in my head. I'm supposed to suck it up and turn it off, turn away from temptation and back to my husband who loves me even if it's quiet, who shows it in subtle ways, whom I love and respect and sleep next to and with each night in our bed in our house with our three young children we made who are sleeping in their beds, our three young children who know only our love and laughter, who do not know that strangers can take up residence in dreams and dark bars and computers, how even temptation resisted can cause rifts.

It is no sin to be tempted, but is it one to dwell in temptation, to pick out a dress you know will be flattering to your thinner figure, to want to feel attractive and beautiful after all these years of making babies—swelling and shrinking and swelling and shrinking and swelling and shrinking again—to laugh and then to worry that you are asking for something you don't want, not really, anyway?

❄

Brandon and I plan weekly date nights, or biweekly when it gets too busy, an evening a week when we get to be husband and wife instead of mother and father or employee or chauffeur. During the busy football travel season, it is a life raft for our marriage. We budget for a babysitter and overspend on dinner and drinks, but it is worth it to ride alone together in the car, to sit across from each other over steak and salads and talk about something other than when the kids' next soccer practice is, who will pick them up, what we're cooking for dinner. From the time the sitter arrives until we reluctantly pull in the drive, he is mine, all mine, husband I get to enjoy, husband who opens doors, reaches for my hand, husband who exchanges movie lines and sings song lyrics with me, husband whose feet wander under covers to rub against mine.

"Well, hello," he says, or I say, "Are you *really* tired?"

We drive to Medina for line dancing at the Thirsty Cowboy, this week's date night destination. We drink whiskey together, like we do, and I laugh and sway. I've drunk too quickly to keep up with my body, and it's been a long time since we last line danced. I don't altogether remember the steps, but I can still cha-cha, the rhythm and turn and rock step instinctual on the hardwood. As usual, I wonder if he's watching my body. I wonder if he admires his wife. When Brandon leaves me on my barstool to close our tab, I lean heavy against the bar and watch the older couples waltz, watch the drunk girls dance out of line, watch the regulars soar across the floor as if the dance was invented for them. A twenty-something male approaches on my right. I turn my head and grin, my eyes slow to keep up with the motion of my head.

"Hey there, how are you doing tonight?" he asks with a smile.

"Oh, I'm fine!" I grin toothily. He glances down at my hands, which have taken up their dutiful position of holding up the bar.

"Oh, you're married! I'm sorry," he says, stepping back as if a magnetic field has just been breached, the glint of metal and stone repelling his advance.

I keep grinning, "Yup," I say. Brandon, my knight in shining armor, returns with a clear plastic glass of water and nods at the bashful guy backing away, his hands raised shoulder-level as if to say, *Sorry, I didn't know.*

I snicker, "He was going to hit on me!" I am wide-eyed and still grinning.

"Yup," Brandon says, his hand on the small of my back, "I could tell that's what was happening." He pushes the water my way and I gulp it hungrily. "Ready to go, Tiny Dancer?"

"Uhhmm, yes," I say, "with your assistance." We mosey toward the door, every brain cell and neuron focused on placing one foot in front of the other, ever confident that, even though I *am* drunk, I am an amazing actress, and surely no one, especially not the bouncer checking IDs at the door, has any inclination of how much alcohol I've consumed in this very short time. I grin and say goodnight to him. We walk, my arm wrapped tightly around my husband's waist, his firm grip supporting me all the way to our car, and we drive the highway home, the dark world spinning.

When Brandon leaves for work each weekend, I sit in the quiet of my living room, watch romantic comedies and write, scroll through Facebook posts, and wonder if he'll send me a note. Wonder if he's thinking about me. Either one—Brandon or not-my-husband. There's a YouTube video on his Facebook wall. It's about a girl he wants to see who's far away from him. Him—not-my-husband—not my husband. A message pops up on the screen. "Swells . . . " it says. My fingers hover over the keyboard.

It could be so easy. Look how easy it could be! So easy. So fast. So immediately painless. It could just *happen. How could this happen to me?*

Just weeks before, Brandon and I had returned from Lost River, West Virginia, navigated together nine years of marriage and three children, four miscarriages, three houses, three dogs, career changes, church crises, new friendships, new diets. We spent the trip reminiscing and predicting the future, the bright and uncertain and beautiful future we imagined always with us together. Married. Forever. Love. In love. Totally hot, mountaintop high, West Virginia country roads love.

And then this. Sly words and posts and pictures and songs that all seem to whisper, *I'm over here, I'm thinking of you. All you have to do is say "yes."* It's like a pebble in my shoe; no, eating potato chips at the beach, the risk of gritty sand mixed in with each bite. Each line delivered makes me question whether I actually want this, whether I actually invited this, whether I'm happy with what I have, whether I want something else. *Crunch.* Maybe I'm not as happy as I could be in my marriage. *Crunch crunch.* Maybe I like hearing these things. Maybe I'm flattered. *Crunch crunch crunch.* Why doesn't Brandon say these things to me? Why isn't Brandon flirting with me? Why do other men notice me and my own husband seems oblivious? I slide quickly down the scale of contentment to resentment. Sure, my husband loves me. I know this. But he isn't making me happy. Not right this second.

The trouble is I'm assuming that any other person is responsible for my happiness. No lover, no spouse, no child, no parent—my contentment in life depends upon one person alone. Me. My choices. My faith. My hope for the future. Expecting anyone—spouse included—to fill my every need every minute of the day in order to secure happiness is unreasonable. Selfish. So why go looking elsewhere for someone else to fill your happiness when most of the time, it's *you* who needs to refocus, to find contentment within, peace with God, love for one's self?

Why? Because it's easier. The bag of chips is filled with salt and sand, and it's easier to keep eating than to retrieve a clean bag from the beach house above. Easier right this instant, to text, to message, to poke, to flirt, to feel that thrill of lust and desire, to treat the symptom instead of the disease . . . until you zoom out beyond this instant and focus in on the possible wreckage ahead.

With all of this passive resistance, this loose-armed stop sign and smile, I could be the one to drive us into a guardrail. Even though my husband and I had talked about temptation, about bar scenes and dinners out when he's on the road for work, ("Just so you know, I'm married . . . ") I thought we were talking about him and his temptations. Not me. I am infidelity-proof. I've had three children, after all! This could never happen to me; I love him too much to ever be tempted, value my family and my three children and these painted walls and framed portraits of smiling faces far more than any fling, far more than any other man's advances.

But it hasn't just "happened" to me. Maybe it landed unexpectedly in my lap, or on my thigh, but I am making a choice by allowing it to continue, the flirting and the compliments disguised by friendship in email messages and texts, I let them arrive, I receive them. *Go away,* I say, *Hey, how are you doing,* I say. I have the power to protect my marriage or to maim it beyond recognition, to the point that reconstructive surgery or, God forbid, amputation might be necessary. *I* am a threat.

It is date night again. We take the county roads to Paradise Hills, a cow pasture of a golf course, and walk the back nine. The light on the course in autumn is golden and we squint. In the rays of the setting sun, it's impossible to think or aim and so I swing my driver by instinct, hear the club connect with the ball, the whistle of it sailing through the air, and try to shield my eyes to see where it lands, but it is lost in the light.

"Nice shot," Brandon says, and we carry our clubs toward the greens, walking a yard or two apart. "You have to swing the pitching wedge a little harder there to get it out of the rough," he says.

Ten years ago, we golfed together for the first time. I giggled and pranced around the tee box, gripped my club too tight, broke my wrists, dipped when I swung, and gophered the ball across the rough.

"It's all in the hips," I teased, swaying back and forth. This is the way I had behaved with other boys, golf something like foreplay until the cover of night could be drawn. It seemed to be what the boys wanted: a sexy caddy in a polo shirt, not an actual competitor.

"You need to keep your eye on the ball," Brandon instructed. "Do you even want to play better?" I wasn't really interested in playing better. I was interested in getting and keeping his attention, taking a long walk under the sycamores, admiring the landscaping job the maintenance crew had done. Golf was an accessory. "Bend your knees. Keep your arms straight. The tee is too low in the ground."

"It's all in the hips," I grinned.

Ten years later, we walk the course together. I adjust my stance, judge the distance between me and the greens, take a practice swing, and listen. Silence. Brandon watches. I stop choking the club, inhale, bend my knees and swing, rotating at the waist, pacing the pull back and follow through like a pendulum, connect and watch the ball lift into sunlight.

"Nice one," Brandon says, smiling, "It's all in the hips."

"I have found you pretty darn compelling, Sarah Wells," he says after a dozen or more safe back-and-forths about the writing life one afternoon at work. It burns in my gut and rushes to my cheeks, my nerve endings flare. I don't know what to say, so I cut off the thread with a smiley-faced emoticon and "I try." *I try?* That's what I type? I am trying all kinds of things. I write blog posts about temptation and resisting temptation, loaded with Bible verses I've used to buttress myself, verses I've prayed through and wrestled with and clung to that he's replied to, "Thanks for throwing all those Bible verses at me." I'm trying. Trying to maintain a work friendship. Trying to avoid a scandal. Trying to be engaged with my kids. Trying to love my husband. Trying to keep up appearances. Trying to keep all of the pieces together, separate. Trying to do it alone.

❊

On a night I'm feeling particularly insecure, particularly needy, remembering the flirtatious exchanges on Facebook and email that have dwindled at my request, I wait for the compliments from my husband. I look for his gaze to settle a little while longer on my figure, dissect every distracted glance away from our conversation. Nothing meets my expectations. I want him to admire me, say sweet things about my body. I even ask, "What is it you love about me?" and he doesn't know how to answer.

"You know I'm not good at this kind of thing." He sits back on the couch, exasperated. I stand up and storm around the kitchen, stomp down the basement stairs to switch loads, itching for something, anything, to distract me. Brandon comes downstairs.

"What's the matter with you?"

I swallow and sigh. I want to say, "Nothing," to stay cold and safe in my carapace of indifference. I want to say, "I'm fine." I don't want to confess my neediness. It all feels so self-absorbed, this desire to be adored, this hunting for signs of love. I lift the damp clothes from the washer and fling them into the dryer, avoiding his question.

"Stop doing laundry and look at me."

I should trust this man by now. He loves me. I know this. We have known each other for ten years and still the fear boils in me that I will be denied the right to feel, that my emotions will be discarded as wrong, that something will short circuit in our conversation, he will deflect and accuse me of always making him out to be the bad guy, launch into a tirade of past hurts and offenses. I have known plenty of men who have done this.

But not my husband.

He has always considered my words, swallowed them and digested them, humbled himself and answered with love, even when he doesn't understand, incredulous that I could think such things or feel so low, even faced with the ugliest side of me. And yet here I am, avoiding the opportunity to tell him how I feel, how his words can shore up my borders, protect, serve as ammunition in the silent, needy moments, when the living room is dark and I am alone, approaching lonely.

I finish the load of laundry and face him. I feel like I look hungry, hopeful, afraid.

He puts his hands on either side of my face and our eyes connect. "I love how much you love God. You are a great mother and an amazing wife. I love how patient you are with the kids and with me. I love how you make me feel loved and needed." These are not the words I had expected, and my heart cracks open, my throat closes. I sob and tremble. He continues on as he holds me, whispers reasons in my ear, reasons why he loves me, reasons that have nothing to do with my body and everything to do with *me*. He loves *me*.

"I had to unfriend someone on Facebook," I tell Brandon over drinks one night at a bar in Pittsburgh. His crew is working the noon game Saturday, and Pittsburgh is close enough to drive. The kids are with our parents, and it's just us. We just finished dinner and debated dessert while we drank, talking about Facebook and hiding annoying posts by people we hardly know. This is the first time I have felt compelled to say something to him about not-my-husband.

"Really? Who?" he asks, and I tell him.

"Why?"

"He was saying things he shouldn't, and I needed to stop it," I say, aloof, smiling, as if I am not reeling inside, this thing that caused me to unfriend a friend clearly not penetrating the fortress I've built around my heart.

"Wow," he says. "Okay. I don't know what to think about that." I smile, and we each take a sip of our drinks, look in opposite directions. I don't know that I can say anymore. He doesn't ask, and I don't continue.

But it continues, random moments when an email turns from professional to flirtatious, sudden reminders when a Google chat window pops open, quiet times weeks apart when I remember what he said and it quakes and lurches in my gut.

I tell Lisa. I tell another friend. I tell another friend. "Nothing has happened," I say, "but he won't go away. I want him to go away."

I hear, "He is an arrogant asshole."

"Yes, but, I *liked* to hear those things, so what am I supposed to do with that?"

I hear, "Wow, Sarah, I'm sorry that's been happening."

"I don't think I can have male friends."

I hear, "You are strong."

"I would rather walk around with my heart on empty occasionally," I blather, "than fill it with this grit." Each one is a rope thrown to a rescuer in case I start to fall.

An innocent email takes a turn. Sometimes I poke the bear, *Hey, how are you doing?* hoping it will just be friendly banter again. Sometimes the messages come unprovoked. It persists, even after an email plea, please, respect my marriage and my family, which feels a little silly, a little over-dramatic. But I know my weakness.

"Oh Swells," he writes back an hour later, "It's all games. Fear not." I blink and stare at the screen. It is after the workday is over, and I keep his reply open on my phone, glance at it every minute or two as I pick up my kids from the sitter, a pizza from Little Caesar's.

As the kids and I eat dinner forty-five minutes later, I reply, "Just making sure we are clear."

Why couldn't I just take these little asides as "all games?" Why did they feel like such a huge threat to me? I find myself wondering if I've built this all up in my head on this side of the computer, if I've made this into an untamable monster when really, it's just a silly puppy playing tricks and pulling strings. Have I imagined this pursuit to be more than what it actually is? And if so, why? Why am I wired this way? Why is maintaining this friendship and evading his affection so important to me? How could other women not even blink an eye while mine widen in shock, while I recoil and run as if I am Joseph standing in Potiphar's wife's bedroom, fleeing from a lustful advance as if my life depended on it?

Maybe it's because my life depends on it. Everything in my life I value depends upon me fleeing. I can see the tender places where I bruise easily. Doesn't it make sense, then, to run away from what I know is a certain stumbling block, to take the flat asphalt path instead of the sidewalk interrupted by the roots of trees pushing the concrete up in uneven steps? It doesn't matter if other women can take it in stride, accept the advances of other men without it affecting their marriages. I can't.

❋

On a weekday night after a spring softball game, Brandon goes out with the guys to eat wings, drink beer, and sing karaoke. He comes home late and wakes me up. He is shaking.

"You know Hannah, Lisa's friend? You remember meeting her, right?"

"Yes," I mumble, still blinking away the sleep, "I remember her." When we met Hannah last summer, I could tell there was chemistry between them. I teased him afterward about it.

"She was there tonight, and she was coming on to me. I told the guys to keep her away from me. Nothing happened," he starts to weep and shudder, "Your essay about resisting temptation was posted just this morning and here I am, in a bar, with a girl I find attractive, and I understand now, I understand," he says, and I am wide-eyed at this strange timing, this strange mercy, this strange grace.

In the morning, Lisa sends a text, "Before he left the bar he told me to never bring Hannah around him again. You have a great man."

I'm nervous when he comes back to town. It's been a year. I can feel it creeping up my chest, even though I feel confident there is no way I will betray Brandon. There is no way. I worry that it won't matter. Maybe in a weak moment, not-my-husband, whose emails still sting in half-truths and one-liners, who says he would never do anything to hurt me because "You're so good, and I know it would destroy you," who says he is looking forward to seeing me, "Is that okay?", maybe he would disregard the things I've said and try something anyway. Maybe in a moment in a bar after we've had a few to drink, our spirits blurred, he would forget.

I want to know for myself that I am strong enough, that the temptation is dead, or at the least, just a little puppy. I want to prove to myself that I am master of my emotions, I am in control. I am also stupid and curious and afraid and confident. Brandon is out of town; the kids are with my in-laws. We go for drinks in a bar that's brightly lit this time, with other people around. His hand travels toward my thigh and again I say, "No!" again I push his hand away, and he smiles sheepishly. The bartender is younger, and I wonder if she thinks there's something going on here. Does the rest of the bar also think the same, do any of these people know me, have they seen me, do they know my husband and know that this is not my husband and know that I am my husband's wife and what is she doing in this bar with this man who keeps trying to touch her thigh, and why is she smiling like that? My nerves are on edge. I am smiling to hide it.

Nothing has changed on his end, except his wife has issued him divorce papers. I'm sorry for him, sorry they didn't make it work. But what do I know about their marriage? I only know about *my* marriage. He has a new girlfriend. This is really good news for him and for me, except he's still here, and I'm still here, with his wandering hand, without his wedding band. Because I invited him out to talk. Because we're just friends.

Why am I here again? I drink my Smirnoff Ice. I wasn't going to order whiskey; I drink whiskey too quickly. I ask about his new girlfriend. He shows me her picture and adores her and then looks at me and groans and then looks at her picture again. He asks how things are between me and Brandon, and I tell him they are good; it was a rough spring with a busy travel season, but things are good now. They *are* good. I *love* my husband. I remind him that my story has not changed—I have always loved my husband. He doesn't believe that I am happy for him and his new girlfriend; he doesn't believe that I do not want him. I *do* want him—I want him to be a friend again. I want to step into his car and not wonder whether he will reach over the armrest. I want to be normal around him and not worry that he is taking everything I do as flirtatious, desirous.

We leave the bar. He drives me around. I don't want to go home, but I don't want to keep leading him on. I guess that's what I'm doing, too, leading him on. The trouble is he's still fun to talk to, fun to laugh with, fun to drink with, still a friend, I guess, and maybe I'm just being ridiculous, just being naïve, just being weak. All of this rolls around my brain as we drive. I'm still grinning, still amazed that any other man could be so taken by me, *me.*

This is the tension between my brain and soul, body and spirit warring.

He keeps saying he wants to kiss me, just once, just to see what it would be like. He thinks it's amazing that I haven't kissed anyone since I met Brandon. Not once has it ever occurred to me to kiss another person besides my husband.

"I bet it would be great, I bet we would be great together," he says. We pull in my driveway. I hesitate.

I wonder if the neighbors are looking out their living room window. My heart races. What if they are? What would they think? What would they assume about me sitting in this car with not-my-husband? I rest my head upon my knees and groan. *How do I keep letting this happen?* I pray, *What am I doing here, Lord. I don't want this man. I don't want to destroy my life. Help me.* Not-my-husband starts to rub my back and my muscles relax. I feel my body wanting more, loosening. This frightens me.

Suddenly a voice loud and true roars through every nerve and I hear it clear as the night sky, clear as anything I've ever known or heard, *Get out of this car, Sarah, get out now!*

I throw open the passenger door, "I have to get out of here," I say, stepping out in a rush, "I'll see you later."

He doesn't want to be just friends. He can't.

In that moment, something snaps. Whatever had a hold on me relaxes and I am free, suddenly so free, unburdened of this fear, strong against this man, any man, every man. No more. Never again. I skip quick from brick to brick on the path my husband laid across the lawn early this winter so we wouldn't have to trudge in the sludge made from melting snow in the grass, skip up the front steps and through the front door and into the darkened living room where our marriage photo hangs framed in bright white. My veil is lifted and draped behind my head, alight from afternoon sun. Brandon angles inward toward me and my shoulder tucks under his in the picture as the headlights sweep across our front window, pause and then spread across the lawn, across the maples, arcing like a pendulum swing and then away down Morgan Avenue. I do not watch him pull away.

Brandon and the kids come home from his parents' house and we take a short walk. It is tomorrow. The afternoon is sunny and mild; it is summer but the weather is behaving like fall. The leaves on the trees rustle and stir. Henry is marching down the sidewalk, pumping his arms and throwing his feet out in front of him to try to keep up with his siblings. Lydia and Elvis race each other to the white bench around the tall pin oak, squeal and giggle and glow. Everything is glistening, everything is shining, everything is reflecting light that penetrates my breastbone so that my chest aches, burns my eyes so that I have to squint in order to see. So much could be lost in the glare. Mercy is everywhere.

No more. Never again, I repeat in my head, so free I feel like I'm emitting rays of light refracted through shattered glass. I know the depths of these cracks. Daily, there will be decisions, daily, I have a choice. *No more. Never again.* I reach for Brandon's hand and squeeze.

From Above and Below

Dad and I sat on the tailgate of his truck and waited. My skinny shins swung back and forth rhythmically and unconsciously, a child not yet woman, always in motion. The night air was warm enough to be out without a coat. The maple on the hill cast a dim shadow from the light of the moon.

"Oh! There's one! Did you see it?" I asked, pointing to the sky. The Perseid meteor shower was supposed to be clearest in the darkest of night. It was still early, by that standard, but already the falling stars had begun to dash across the sky. Each one sent a jolt to my heart. "Wow," I said. "So beautiful."

The tip of Dad's cigarette glowed orange in the night. He took a draw and then exhaled the smoke off to the side away from me. Summer's night sounds surrounded us, a silence that was everything but silent, a silence whirring with the hum of insects, the rustle of summer leaves, our breathing in and out.

In the middle of the silence, we watched the sky and waited for more flickering, fleeting glimpses of a space beyond our world.

Brandon and I sneak out the patio doors of our bedroom and sit in the tall wooden beach chairs to watch the ocean and the sky as the Perseid meteor shower begins. There isn't much to see from the second-floor deck except the sky and the shoreline spotted with outdoor lights, a hint of the horizon line in the distance. The ocean pushes rhythmically against the sand, looming mysterious below. From where we sit and with the limited amount of light, we can't see the beach clearly, but we can hear it, a constant swelling and crashing reminder of its presence.

This body of water that already seems endless and huge in daylight only grows in its mystery after the sun has set. In the darkness of night, what rages onshore is unknown. The waves could be monstrous or simply lapping the sand, it's hard to tell. The sand itself seems to move and sink and rise overnight as the ocean works its shifting. In the morning, we would walk along the shoreline and find the castles and moats that were created yesterday swept away, no evidence left except maybe a small whirlpool, some discarded shells. The ocean daily restores the beach, undoing what has been done.

I don't care to walk along the shoreline at night. I want only to sit near the roar of the ocean, the warm salt breeze gusting, and revel in this power and this glory, both above us and below, to hear the work of redemption on the shore. We sigh and watch the sky.

From far above the push and pull, the tension I had carried in my shoulders for what felt like forever loosens. I am free, free, free at last. *I only stopped because you told me to,* he had said in his final text, and I checked delete. Done. Gone. Away. It was as if it had been a year of low tide, the beach pummeled by wind, pockmarked by strangers building castles in the sand, setting up camp with their beach umbrellas and chairs, pounding the packed and broken shells with their tennis shoes in the morning and excavating the beach for what lay hidden underneath at night, all with no relief, no high tide to wash away the wreckage of the day. Until now.

The meteor shower was just beginning, brief and sudden flashes of shooting stars across the broad sky. "Look!" I point and shout, expecting the latest gleam to flicker out to nothing quick, but "Oh!" it keeps going, a long tail of fire streaking against the black, burning through the atmosphere, as if it might never fizzle out, as if it might stretch and burn and fall, on fire, until it lands with a great splash in the ocean. I grab my husband's arm and grin.

With every crash against the shoreline, a surge of gratitude moves within my chest, washing away what had been done, a few divots in the surface, some minor pools in craters.

Here I am. I am here.

I sit with him on the beach chairs high above all of those unknowns holding his hand, staring out over the dunes and up into the night sky. The beach will be flat again tomorrow, the waters edged in—this far, and no more.

I am grateful for the roar.

A Car to Drive

I WAS RAISED IN a safe place. The world around me posed no threats; it was mostly trees, mostly fields, mostly family. Our family played bluegrass music, picked fieldstones from cultivated soil, sowed seedlings with a garden hoe and hand trowel, helped to bring in the harvest whether it was corn or wheat or hay. I learned the word "culture" in fifth grade but struggled to find a meaning for it with no person, place, or thing that was different from what I knew, only rumors of musicians and movies beyond the world of folk and country I was raised in, and that world was anxiety-free, threat-free, easy living riding on bicycles down dirt road back streets, keys left in the ignition of the unlocked truck. I lived, as Tim McGraw sings, where the green grass grows.

It was through my cousins that I learned the reach of pop culture: oversized New Kids on the Block buttons pinned to their blue jeans, Duck Hunt and Mario on their new Nintendo, and sweet smelling Cabbage Patch Kids like real babies, dusted in powder. In winter, we figure skated on the flooded field behind their home to "Ice, Ice, Baby" blaring on the battery-powered boombox balanced on a milk crate. But most of the time, we listened to and recorded music off of "Cleveland's own country music radio station," WGAR, especially the evening show, "Cryin', Lovin', or Leavin'." That was the definition of living given by country radio: the adults were crying over each other, loving one another, or leaving.

I didn't know anything about those things. They happened under the cover of darkness, my mom packing us up into the car, intermittent street-lights flashing past our window—where were we going without Dad that night—was Mom crying, loving, or leaving? I sang along anyway, moments like this in memory's shadows, so few and far between I struggle to recall them. These were adult things, and in our house until I was a teenager, they stayed behind the closed bedroom doors. When they seeped between the floorboards and the door, their presence was eclipsed by silence, long charcoal smears of silence.

My cousins and I waited for our favorites, like "Chains" by Patty Loveless or maybe "Dumas Walker" by The Kentucky Headhunters. For years I thought Patty sang, "Chains, chains, checkers and chains" (*shackles and chains*) and the Headhunters, "Let's all goooo, out to do Miss Walker," which, upon adult reflection, was a fairly terrible mondegreen ("Dumas Walker" is the name of a retail shop that sold beer . . . and "slaw, burger, fries, and a bottle of 'Ski"). Later, we'd create our own call-in show using the Little Tikes toy microphone, "Are you cryin', lovin', or leavin'?" then press play, David Lee Murphy's "Party Crowd" crackling through the cassette tape.

"Tonight I'm looking for a car to drive," I croon with David Lee Murphy.

"What did you just sing?" my husband asks.

"You heard me—tonight I'm looking for a car to drive . . . "

"It's 'party crowd,' not 'car to drive,'" he laughs.

Look how long I've been singing it wrong.

He Thinks He'll Keep Her

I HAVE GOTTEN A lot of mileage out of sweet potatoes. Those suckers are hard to slice. Push the knife blade through, again and again. You have to use both hands, one on the handle and another on the blade. We prepare these sweet potato fries at least once a week, Brandon and I. He sits in the olive green folding chair on one side of the kitchen while I slice. The thump of the knife against the cutting board cracks and vibrates throughout the room. The knife slides against the flesh of the potato like leaflets of paper turned against each other, pages of a book rustled then ripped from the spine . . . *Shhhhh crack. Shhhhh crack.*

It's what I'd like to do with days from the last year, tear them off the calendar, all of the moments I worried over emails that turned from professional to suggestive, the misinterpreted hugs and smiles, the attempts my colleague made to kiss me, the times I hid my phone and laptop, afraid he would send a message and Brandon might see it. It has been a full year and a half since the first incident at a bar, his hand on my thigh and my shocked grin, "No! You have to stop touching me!" It has been months since my loose-armed protests asking him to stop saying all the right things.

It was the wrong man speaking those words. I had spent months navigating my own temptations, worrying over whether I had asked for it, whether I actually wanted it, whether I was unhappy in my marriage, whether I was sending some unspoken signal to him that said "yes" when all my lips kept saying was "no." When he finally stopped after one last attempt during the summer, one last hand on the thigh, one last back rub, one last text that said, "I only stopped because you told me to," one year after he first confessed his crush, I exhaled. Phew. Done.

It's December now. Just a few days ago, I left Human Resources training trembling. During the session I texted Brandon—"You were right, it was sexual harassment."

Oh.

"Do you think I've overreacted?" I ask my husband as I cut the sweet potatoes. *Shhh crack. Shhh crack.* He sits in the folding chair on the other side of the kitchen, and I face the opposite direction, cutting and cutting. "Maybe I blew it all out of proportion, maybe it was all in my head."

The space between us expands into miles, me on a volcanic island, him on a distant shore. Until recently, the most I had said to Brandon about my colleague was, "He's still a problem." I couldn't give him details; I didn't want to hurt him, and I thought I could handle it on my own. After the training session, I had to tell him more, all.

"I mean, I know you said that it was a 'kick in the balls.' But I don't know what that means." I keep cutting, facing away. We tell each other everything, now. Maybe he's shocked that someone like my colleague, the man who knew my family and shook hands with my husband before putting his hand on my leg, would have the balls to touch me like that. Maybe he thinks I wanted it. Maybe he thinks I should have been stronger. Maybe he thinks being out with a colleague for a couple of drinks without him meant I was looking for something more, something more than just friends. Maybe he doesn't think the flatteries, the hand on my thigh, his attempts to kiss me, the emails, all from my colleague over the course of a year, maybe he doesn't think they were sexual harassment. Maybe I'm just being naïve.

What I want to know and die to ask but just can't say: Was I right to be angry at my colleague, was I right to feel enraged after so long feeling just ashamed, aware I hadn't been firm enough, strong enough, to say no completely and utterly? How does it make him feel to know his wife was so conflicted, distracted, insistent, for so long, keeping these thoughts to herself so as not to hurt him, to try to take care of things alone? *I got this. I can handle this. I will handle this,* I had thought. And I had: in some ways, I was proud, victorious, *Yes!* I wanted to shout, I *resisted.*

Here I stand, now, in my kitchen. Maybe he thinks I've blown this out of proportion. Maybe he thinks I flirted with leaving. Maybe he blames me for not being strong.

"I do have some questions," he says softly.

I turn to him. "Like what?"

He hesitates, looking down into his palms. "I just ... "

"I was never interested in leaving, if that's what you need to know," I blather quickly. "I have thought this over time and time again. I wasn't looking for anything. It caught me off-guard, but I never doubted us. I never doubted." My voice shakes. Brandon sits in athletic shorts and a t-shirt still looking down at his hands. He looks like he did back in the days after he broke up with me, before we were engaged. No man had ever looked so sad.

I told not-my-husband that life was good between Brandon and me, even when I caught myself wondering if it would be easier if we just separated, less emotionally draining. It wasn't his business what was actually happening in my marriage. He needed to believe things were great. Any less than "great," and the floodgates might break. Those days my kids said my name multiple times before they caught my attention. I walked in a haze of anxiety—*What if the next email I send to him turns flirtatious again?*—I thought, *What if he's still thinking of me; is he still thinking of me?*

"You said you were confused, that you wondered why you wore a certain kind of dress," Brandon mumbles.

"I know. When he texted me that he kept thinking about me in that dress, it confused me," I stutter, "that he would say he found me attractive." I changed out of my dress pants and blouse when I got home today and slipped into warm-up pants and a t-shirt, something comfortable. I tuck the strands of hair around my face behind my ears.

I wondered why I chose the dress because I've wondered why I dress up for anything, who is it that I'm trying to impress, why does it matter whether I look pretty or professional or fashionable or frumpy, does it matter? Did I think to myself, I look good in this dress, so I will wear it? Yes. Did I choose the dress because I thought *he* would like it? No. Did his response to my dress make me worry that I chose it for him, after the fact? Yes.

But I didn't.

"Anyway, it doesn't matter. I am so sorry, Brandon," I'm bawling now. "I'm so sorry, because I didn't know; I just didn't *know* what was happening." Our children sleep soundly in their beds upstairs, fans roaring for white noise. The sliced sweet potatoes wait to be tossed with olive oil on the counter.

"Why are you apologizing?" he asks.

"Nothing happened, but all of that nothing wrecked an entire year. I hate how off my priorities were." Our eyes are locked, now, even from this distance across the kitchen. "I was so worried about preserving friendships, keeping silent so I didn't cause a scene, holding the status quo, being *nice*, that I failed to protect what is most important here. You. Us. Our family. What we've built. That is what kills me. I'm so sorry. I'm so sorry." I can't stop saying it, *I'm so sorry.*

Brandon looks down for a moment and then up again at me. "I forgive you, for whatever it is that you feel like you need to apologize for. I love you," and then the land masses we stand on collide. We hold each other long in the kitchen, tears falling heavy on each other's shoulders, kissing the tears away, salt strong on our lips.

"I'm sorry I haven't tried hard enough. To love you," Brandon mumbles. I start to shake my head, start to say, *no*, try to say, *shhh, it's okay*. But of course it isn't okay. "Old wounds hang around a long time," Brandon whispers into my shoulder. Yes, they do; gaps and scars our neurons build around and bind, habits developed, survival mechanisms that engage even under the slightest threat.

Ten years earlier, before we were engaged, we argued in the car. I must have just said something about wanting to make more time to spend together, longing to see him in the midst of the never-ending sports seasons, a conversation that has looped again and again during the last decade.

I looked at him. "I never asked you to quit these things. I love this part of you. I love *all* of you. But you have to know that I need your time and attention, too. I want to be a part of your life, a part of you." His ex-fiancée wasn't interested in his passion for competition. My ex-boyfriend wouldn't have heard these words, these needs. How long I had wanted someone to want me. We drove on, the ghosts of our pasts leaning their heads between us from the backseat, staring and accusing.

It takes twenty-two minutes for our sweet potatoes to bake in the oven at high heat. Steam lifts from the back of the stovetop. I run my hands over Brandon's freckled face, through his dark hair, seasoned with silver now, trace again and again the lines of this man I love so much, this man I hurt, this man.

"I am so sorry that I forgot your birthday," Brandon says into my shoulder in the kitchen, "Well . . . I didn't forget. That I didn't get you something."

I smile. "It doesn't matter; it wouldn't have mattered any other time."

He flinches. "Yes. Poor timing."

My birthday, months earlier, was the last of dozens of minor moments I had felt like his last priority, loved well enough as the mother of our three children, appreciated on occasion, but no longer romanced. I was worn thin, proud one minute for standing up against temptation and hollow the next, waiting for some action by my husband, some statement that would confirm I was worth fighting for. *Don't you think I am lovely?* I wanted to ask, but what good would that do except force him into an answer?

It wasn't fair, though, to wait for these compliments to come, to wait for him to stand up. I hadn't said a word except, "He's still a problem," no context or details, no mention of physical contact or contents of emails. During the birthday dinner I planned at "our" restaurant, The Cabin, we exchanged diplomatic words about how I should have said something sooner about my colleague, I should have done something earlier, I should have put a stop to it all. How could I, though, when I didn't know that what he had been doing wasn't provoked? *Did I ask for it,* I still wondered? How to express my confusion, how to word properly the desire to avoid a scandal, how to say I wanted to stay friends with that man, that colleague? There was no way.

Dinner slowly deteriorated. We paid the bill and drove home in the dark, headlights catching and throwing shadows that threatened on either side of the road, shadows encroaching on our car, shadows that skittered away on our approach but followed close to the taillights all the way home.

The stress caused me to snap in our bedroom: "You were gone six days," I sobbed. "Six days, out of town, and you didn't think to plan anything or buy anything for me. You can plan golf outings weeks in advance, you can plan nights out with your friends, you can stay up late and drink and laugh and sing karaoke with Jerry, you can order yourself a new golf club or a magazine subscription or a baseball bat or any other number of things, but you can't think for one minute about me? You say I'm a priority, but I am not a priority here. I am the low man on the totem pole. I try to be understanding, I try to give you space because I know this is your break from work, but I need to feel loved, and I do not feel loved, Brandon. I don't."

It was quiet after that. I curled against the mattress facing the wall in our bedroom, buried under our quilt.

"You just called me out on a lot of things," he said, "and you are right about all of them. I'm so sorry, Sarah." I wanted to say *it's okay.* It'd be okay. It had to be okay. But I stayed silent. "Do you want me to leave?" he asked.

"No!" I said, "The opposite! I want you to love me!" Isn't that the opposite of leave? How had he come to that conclusion? Maybe he wanted me to leave. Maybe he wanted to be let off the hook, free from this commitment. Maybe this was too much work. Maybe I was too hard to love.

"Do you want *me* to leave?" I asked.

"No, Sarah, of course not," and then he was next to me on our bed. "I love you so much, more than you could possibly know."

That was the trouble; I didn't know, I couldn't know. Nothing he had been doing, except sticking around, except being a good father, felt like he loved me. I knew in my head, *yes, he loves me*, of course *he loves me*, but. Can't I know more than that? Can't I *feel* it, too, can't I feel desired?

"I love you, too," I whispered, "But I'm not ready to forgive you."

The next morning, I texted Lisa from the bathroom, still exhausted from our fight. *Even A-hole got me a chocolate bar.* I had joked with him, *I'd love a chocolate bar.* I had asked for it. He had brought it. I left my phone on the counter and sat down with Henry on the couch in the living room.

Brandon stood in the entryway of the living room and asked, "He gave you a chocolate bar?"

My face flushed. "Yes," I said, realizing where I left my phone. It was the first tangible piece of evidence given against not-my-husband, and Brandon ran with it, competition boiling in his blood.

There were chocolates at dinner that night, a stuffed bear and a bouquet of flowers, a note with a line from "Angel Eyes," a John Hiatt song. I rolled my (angel) eyes. Chocolates? A teddy bear? Flowers? Is that the best you can do?

When we were first married, I persuaded Brandon to work through a nightly marriage devotional. We lay underneath blankets in our bed, and before he could roll over and begin snoring, I grabbed the book from my nightstand. He rolled his eyes. *How do you receive love?* The question of the night asked. This was an easy one for me: quality time, lots and lots of quality time, and physical touch, not just sex—although that was important, too—but hugs and kisses, and also compliments, tell me I'm beautiful, tell me you love me, tell me you appreciate me.

"How about you?" I probed.

"I don't know," Brandon squirmed. "When you do things for me, I guess, like pack my lunch."

"Pack your lunch?" I laughed. "Really? That isn't romantic at all."

"This is stupid," he said, rolling over.

The next day at work, he handed me a velvet bag, and in it a ruby necklace, "Your birthstone," he said, and another note, this time, a poem,

> *The glowing ruby shall adorn,*
> *Those who in July are born;*
> *Then they'll be exempt and free,*
> *From love's doubts and anxiety.*
> *Happy birthday to my lovely and beautiful wife. Brandon.*

There was that word, lovely, and the other one, beautiful, the one I hunted for and hoped for to come tumbling out of his mouth, and there it was, right there on the notecard. I folded the note and put it in my purse. I smiled, "Thanks, it's beautiful," still unmoved.

I woke one morning that week with a Mary Chapin Carpenter song blaring in my head. It rested heavily; its lyrics wouldn't stop spinning. The song, "He Thinks He'll Keep Her," scared me.

My life was summarized in the first few verses. *I married Brandon at twenty-one. I said forever, confident in "till death do us part." At twenty-nine, I delivered baby number three.* Every Christmas card shows our family, sometimes all of us, sometimes just the children, always happy, always grinning, a brightly lit tree and fireplace in the background. But there were more verses, verses for the days that loomed ahead of us. I was only five years away from the woman in the song, confessing to her husband that she didn't love him anymore.

Brandon was gone more than he was home that spring. The kids played sports and went to school and I worked and went to conferences and we visited grandparents and celebrated birthdays, us—the four of us—while he worked out of town. Skype is not always enough. Texts are not always enough. Phone calls are not always enough. The time between the brief arrivals and quick departures is not always enough. *I miss you* is true, but sometimes the frustration and the stress outweighs the felt absence. Could we fall apart? Could we separate?

No, I love my husband. No, that will never happen. Will it? Can these promises unravel?

I have always been sure about marriage, the ideal of a deep, committed, transformative, dynamic relationship built in order to bear burdens and share delights with another human being, the same human being, who is able to look back on months and then years and then decades of life and say, "Wow. Can you believe what we've done? Together?"

In 2003, I married Brandon. I uttered vows and made promises; we exchanged rings; we took communion together on our knees, blood and body broken for us, for the forgiveness of sins. We committed to this forgiveness.

We committed to love one another. For better. For worse. In sickness. In health. Till death. I did not slink down the aisle shy; I strode, grinning, confident, my father on my arm and my soon-to-be husband in my sights, the one *I* had chosen to love, the one who had chosen to love *me*. We danced to "True Companion" by Marc Cohn, declaring that we were each other's true companion.

I celebrated my thirty-first birthday that week. *Mary Chapin Carpenter, I desperately want to love my husband still in five years,* I thought to myself, *love him deeper and truer, daily, not temporarily. I am terrified that this love, this family we have built, could fall apart.*

When we first married, we read that "Two are better than one, because they have a good return for their labor: If either of them falls down, one can help the other up. But pity anyone who falls and has no one to help them up . . . " The author of Ecclesiastes continued, "Though one may be overpowered, two can defend themselves. A cord of three strands is not quickly broken." I thought this braid of husband, wife, and God was something firm and unshakeable, but it turned out that its bond is tenuous, capable of loosening quickly, suddenly, a braid whose strands I pull but the hair is too shiny to hold, and the braid unravels. I comb it out and begin again, cross husband over wife, pull God from underneath and wrap around the other two, then wife over husband over God and repeat this weave until it holds, for a time. And then the slow unravel again.

Marriage is filled with opportunities for delight, pleasure, laughter, excitement, and surprise, and in the gaps between lie the threats. Shadows. Terrors. Temptations. Ghosts. Our own weaknesses and tendencies toward disaster, selfishness, addiction. They are *always* there. There is no fully barricaded marriage. I could keep walking quietly in the sunlight, eyeing those shadows, shimmying away from the ghosts. But they will creep up behind me, always.

It had taken him a while to decide back when we were dating, but once he had made up his mind, there was no way Brandon would fall out of love. He isn't that kind of man. Love doesn't just happen, and the falling out doesn't either. My ex-boyfriend from a decade ago, whom I had prayed to be delivered into my arms, whom I had begged to love me, bended for, transformed for in order to be loved, Eric didn't know what happened; he had fallen out of love with me. "It just happened," he said. "I wish I knew why but I don't. Love you. I'm sorry, I don't love you anymore."

The week of my birthday pushed on until Friday night. It had been a long week of work, hours that started at 8:30 in the morning and ended well after nine at night, but I survived, slumped tired onto the couch.

"Here, this is for you," he said. It was a Kindle Fire, and another note, *Love is patient, love is kind, love never fails, B.*

This gift giving was unprecedented in our marriage. Brandon had never been the gift giving type, and I had never really needed gifts, either. We mocked jewelry and holiday commercials, *Where's my BMW with a red bow, honey?* and gave each other concert tickets, restaurant gift certificates, things that we could do together. I loved the necklace, the Kindle, and the gifts that came later, too—a new putter for our fall golf date nights, an iPod for working out at the gym—but it was the notes I valued most, treasured, carry around with me still, so I might feel their softened edges in my purse as I rummaged for change or a pen, something to make a mark.

"Okay, I forgive you," I said with a grin and snuggled up next to him. He kissed my hair. Love never fails.

❧

"You should never have gotten into that car, you know," he says. I stand up to pull the sweet potatoes from the oven.

"Yes," I say, "Yes, that was stupid. But I needed to know. I needed to be sure." The counter ticks down to zero, then beeps.

❧

John Lennon sings *Love, love, love,* in an irregular meter of 4/4 then ¾ then 4/4 time, because as "easy" as love might look, as much as it is "all you need," it's still irregular, unpredictable, utterly complex and layered with other stories and instruments woven together. The song incorporates the French national anthem, elements of "Chanson D'Amour" by Wayne

Shanklin, and orchestral arrangements blending Bach's Brandenburg concerto, Greensleeves, and Glenn Miller's arrangement of "In the Mood."

Just like the song, our love stories are built on the foundation of the ever-afters that preceded us, buttressed by the stories happening around us, and intercepted by the stories developing within us. These songs, they aren't prophetic or prescriptive or didactic. They are reflective. Refractive. Shimmery, even.

Love, love, love. Love, love, love.

She said forever with a smile on her face.

The day of our tenth anniversary, Brandon worked in the TV truck in Blacksburg, Virginia, after we sang karaoke until two in the morning, and I went shopping even though I was worn out. We dressed up and prepared for our dinner reservation. I had been waiting for this afternoon for weeks. Brandon had picked out a ring to replace my cheap engagement ring, the discount stone whose receipt I had discovered after the fact a decade earlier.

"Some mistakes can be corrected," he said the afternoon he went to the jewelers.

I was nervous about it, feeling foolish. *It's still a beautiful ring. I still wore it these ten years. Am I vain? Am I a material girl? Am I worth it?*

I finished applying my makeup and dried my hair in the hotel mirror. "Here, you should wear this tonight," Brandon said quietly, opening the blue velvet box. And there it was, my new ring, five stones across to parallel the five stones in my wedding band. Ten stones for ten years.

"Thank you," I whispered into his shoulder, his warm embrace the safest place I have ever known.

I felt shy and embarrassed at this gift, this extravagance. Brandon handed me an envelope. "It isn't finished yet, but there are chords to it, too," he mumbled as he turned around to fiddle with something on the bed. Maybe he was feeling embarrassed and shy, too.

"You wrote me a song?" I said, tears falling freely.

"Don't cry, you'll mess up your makeup," he said, touching my face, handing me a tissue.

What has passed since my birthday during the summer, since that week of temptations revealed, gifts given? Our ten-year wedding anniversary, singing "Jackson" by Johnny and June at karaoke, the new ring to commemorate a decade, the words Brandon had composed, Sunday trips to Cleveland to watch the Browns lose, date night at The Cabin for dinner, date night golfing, quiet nights at home—Brandon playing his guitar and singing, me typing out stories—fall soccer with the kids, Friday night movie nights without him home, negotiating again the fall football season with him on the road. Normalcy, free from the anxiety of the last year. Months have passed, and here we stand in the kitchen again, closing the gaps, closing the gaps.

"Every time I put on this necklace, every time I slide on this ring, every time I spray the perfume you picked out for me. I remember that I am loved," I say, looking into his eyes, fingering the ruby. We pick up the plate of sweet potato fries and cold bowl of guacamole and head toward the living room.

"Thanks for making the sweet potatoes," he says.

He thinks he'll keep her.

Brandon and Me

"I'M SO EXCITED ABOUT these two weeks," I say over lunch. The residency is here again, the two-week-long writers' party of workshops and craft seminars, readings and bars and karaoke. The last few summers have been tense and uneasy, but this summer, I am ready. I am ready to write, to listen, to pay attention, to be fully present.

"That's great, but be careful. Keep your guard up," Brandon says, looking into my eyes, "It's happened with other men, it could happen again."

I feel the gap where adoration gets trapped expand, and the light leaks out my eyes. "I know," I mumble, "I will be careful," and gather my things to head back to the office. Later, in an email, he explains himself—*You are a beautiful and awesome woman who men will be attracted to even more as you are in your thirties and forties. Just want you to know that. I love you.*

We have this conversation before karaoke night. I am aware of the men in the bar, the men I know and some I don't, the older men who are recently divorced and with younger women, now, the men who watch as I sing Little Big Town's "Pontoon." I am nervous. I haven't had enough to drink to do this, to sing and not notice or care whether there are men watching, what the men are thinking or what they aren't thinking or whether they are watching at all, until Brandon's there, my husband, who laughs and kicks back and gyrates his hips in front of me to get me laughing, too, and he says, "I can do that! I'm her husband!"

We sing together the next round and it's easy as can be, easy, because we're singing and he's next to me. We sing "Jackson," and it's just us. It's us.

"I always assume people know that it's my wife and me," a friend and coworker says. It's Brandon and me. It's always Brandon and me. People should assume that it's Brandon and me.

Home Field Advantage

MY HUSBAND HAS A leather batting glove shoved in the pocket of his baseball pants as he struts and jogs across the field, stoops to field a line drive hit to his position at shortstop. I watch the flick of his shoulder and elbow and wrist, as natural as love, as simple as sunshine, sending the ball back to the pitcher. Baseball pants are my favorite, the way they hug him around the waist, although I miss the socks pulled up to the calves, the stirrup print and pants that begin at the knee. There was something about that cut back when we first began to know each other, hard-bat league games on Tuesday and Thursday and double-header Sundays, but now the pants are long, extending past the ankles over baseball cleats. It's the new style, that and flat-brimmed baseball caps. All the college kids are into them.

He played baseball for thirty years. Now he is thirty-six and swings his bat in a summer softball league. It's *softball*, he scoffs. The games he plays are hour-long double-headers on Wednesdays, and if they play at six I bring the kids. They sprint around the bleachers and climb the stairs and try to pet the frenetic dog and eat other people's treats, and sometimes between the scoldings and warnings I see my husband walk to home plate in those baseball pants with an aluminum bat in hand, watch him step into position, pose and practice swing and pause, wait, pitch, hit, run, safe. I clap and smile. I chase our children around the grounds until they are too tired and miss his circuit around the bases.

When we leave, they cry, "Daddy!"

He walks out of the dugout and lifts them, kisses and hugs goodnight, and turns back to the field. I watch the broad V of his torso, the tweak and flex of his muscles.

In the evenings after the sun sets and our children sleep silently in bedrooms and we flop like heavy dogs on the couch, I study my husband, touch his bristly face, rough after a couple of days without shaving. His skin is tanned and freckled, stretched over bone and muscle he builds and tones at the Y when there's child care, at the hotel's fitness center when he travels. Silver has begun to salt the auburn of his beard, the pepper of his hair, cropped short and trimmed clean along his neck, sideburns short and straight. He threatens to shave his head in order to hide the receding hairline, but I find myself unconsciously reaching for softness, touching the rough places on his cheek, the smooth place around his ears. He closes his eyes and smiles, eyebrows relaxed. I make the rough places smooth.

He flicks from CNN to *MLB Tonight* to reruns of *The Cosby Show* and back to CNN, neat men in business suits with dyed hair broadcasting world news that makes us sad and then angry and then tired. He is warm. I want to be warmer. I work my feet over to where his rest propped on the ottoman, inch across the couch until we are parallel figures in a painting, legs crossed at the ankles, looking in the same direction. I like to rest my head on his chest and turn until I stretch across the couch. Now our bodies are a T. I listen to the rumble of his stomach that overwhelms the beat of his heart and invite his arm around my shoulder. He drapes it across my abdomen, his hand strolling across my chest, teasing down my side so that my body jerks. My arm is falling asleep. A commercial appears and he switches back to ESPN.

"He put that on a tee!" he says, of the pitcher, the baseball gone to souvenir city. We are watching and not watching, eyelids like horizontal blinds opening and closing, drifting and nodding. The announcers roar. The home team just scored.

The Dance: Dad's Lead

FOUR MONTHS BEFORE OUR wedding day, I had come home from college graduation with a boyfriend my parents liked well enough but were still warming to, and an engagement ring. Brandon had asked my dad's permission first, of course, out of my hearing the day before, and Dad had said yes—he hugged me extra-long before I left, cap and gown still on.

In the midst of planning, I asked, "What song do you want to dance to, Dad?" and scrolled through lists of popular father-daughter dance songs.

Nothing seemed right. No Michael Bublé or Paul Simon or Stevie Wonder would cut it; this, after all, was my father—my flannel-shirt-and-faded-blue-jeans, muddy-work-boots, calloused-hands, five-o'clock-shadow, "fetch-me-a-Miller" father. What qualified as "our song"? Maybe "Feed Jake." Maybe "Friends in Low Places." Maybe "Act Naturally." Maybe "There's a Tear in My Beer." Hank and Garth and Buck and the Pirates of the Mississippi sang about misery, friends, beer, and mama; they didn't sing anything about their daughters.

By the day of our wedding, Mom and Dad had settled on a song. "It's a surprise," they said.

In the early planning days, Mom and Dad offered to write us a check: big party vs. down payment on a house. We waffled for a day or two, but in the end, my visions of a white dress and a man in a tux waiting for me won out, dreams of dancing and spinning under a spotlight, all of our friends and family clapping and celebrating.

It was my day to plan, along with my mom, who navigated the wedding planning with me like she was my maid-of-honor. Mom and I picked the flowers—sunflowers and blue delphinium—the same that decorated the cake display we chose. We taste-tested the catering, got weepy-eyed over my bridal gown and veil, and designed the party favors, together. The reception venue was our decision, too, even as my soon-to-be mother-in-law raised her eyebrows and said, "Really, a *barn?*"

Rhonda's choice for the mother-son dance was easy: Louis Armstrong would sing "What a Wonderful World" for thirty seconds and then the record would screech to a stop. Brandon and his mom would look confused for a second until Lou Bega's "Mambo No. 5" would begin to play. It fit them perfectly. After the father-daughter dance to whatever song Mom and Dad had picked, Rhonda and Brandon would get the party started.

I wrote the order of music and communion and rings, I designed the program and inscribed a poem, I recruited our friends as musicians. Brandon and I selected most of the songs and all of the Bible verses for the ceremony. We picked the pastor and the bridal party and the style of music to be played at the reception. We determined the flavor of this wedding, and this wedding would taste just like us.

The guest list: that was *their* decision, the parents, and it grew, and grew, and grew, until we all silently stared at it sitting on the kitchen counter. Who could we possibly cut? No one. Maybe there were a lot of other commitments that weekend, and the guest list would just . . . trim itself. Maybe in *Major League* fashion, we could declare, *This guy here is dead! Cross him off, then!*

Also their decision: the alcohol. We toyed with the idea of a dry wedding for about a twelve-hour timespan because Brandon had just gotten a job at a new school, and we weren't sure yet exactly how conservative they were. A few made Round One of the guest list. It hadn't been decided if they'd make the Round Two cuts.

"You want a *what?!*" Dad asked, his voice rising steadily. "We are not going to invite all of our friends to a wedding and not have alcohol. What kind of a party is that?"

"But, Da-ad," I said, "We just thought, you know, the school . . . and maybe . . . " but it was no use. My excuses were weak, anyway; it wasn't like Brandon and his family and our friends and our relatives never kicked back and drank a glass of wine or a can/six-pack/case of beer, so why pretend otherwise and ruin a good time? Besides, it was Dad's call. Dad's decision. Dad's lead.

So, okay, beer and wine, Dad. And yes, invite *all* of those people, even those people I won't know when they come through the receiving line, and

I'll look at Brandon and he'll look at me, and we'll both smile and shake their hands and give them hugs and thank them for coming. And, okay, yes, pick our father-daughter dance.

❀

Down the aisle we went, Dad in his black tuxedo looking sharp, no John Deere hat to cover his balding head or shadow his features. His hand was tight in mine, tense against a few hundred sets of eyes that watched us while we two-stepped—left together, right together—our paces matched, the Fugman stride slow and easy like a mosey.

I saw only my future husband at the end of the aisle where Brandon waited for me. When we reached the pastor, he asked, "Who gives this woman to be married to this man?"

Dad answered gruffly, "Her mother and I."

I turned my gaze back to him for just that second and wrapped my arms around his neck, and he held on, squeezed and squeezed, then released me to my groom, taking his seat in the sanctuary while I remained standing.

Later, after the bridal dance ended and I parted with a kiss from my new husband, our spunky blue-haired emcee called Dad onto the floor. Dad had donned his Father-of-the-Bride ball cap as soon as the wedding ended and wore it now as he met me for our dance. The bubbles from the bride and groom dance settled and popped on the dance floor. A slow piano, slide guitar, and light percussion played. The cut-time of Mickey Gilley singing "True Love Ways" carried us along the hardwood, Dad's calloused palm in my manicured hand. I smiled, even though the tune was unfamiliar to me. I guess it went to number one on the country charts in 1980, the year my parents started dating. Dad would sing it to her in the car as it played on the radio. *So romantic*, Mom says later. But this was *our* dance, our slow turn under the spotlight. It didn't seem like the right fit—*know true love's ways*—but what would have been?

Earlier in the afternoon, Dad gave me over, his daughter, his only daughter, his dazzled blue-eyed daughter grinning with confidence over the man she had chosen. I came into the sanctuary my father's daughter. I walked out of the sanctuary my husband's wife.

How long had I dreamed of becoming Mrs. Anyone? A boyfriend, a boyfriend, a boyfriend, I wanted one, as long as he would stay around and then another one, and then I wanted that boyfriend to become a fiancé and that fiancé to become my husband, so I could become Mrs. Anyone. In college, that was the title that mattered: I wanted a partner. I wanted someone I could pour my heart into. That's what I thought you did after high school and certainly after college. My mom and dad had grown up across the street from each other; she was nineteen when they married and twenty when she delivered her first baby—me. Today it's ill-advised to marry young, trouble from the start, they don't know what they're getting into, a whole life ahead, plenty of time for that, but from where I stood, I felt behind already.

Yes, I also earned a degree, I also sought out opportunities to lead and to stretch and to achieve, to do more, earn praise, perform. *Fugmans aren't afraid of work, Fugmans are hard workers.* Dad instilled this drive. He was the man who had been my guide. But Brandon was the man I had chosen to walk with me out of the sanctuary, the man who would walk beside me from the altar forward. He brought me a different sort of pride. We had weighed and measured our potential, considered our compatibility, discussed the ways we would raise children, and established our priorities. In him I had found someone I could adventure with, a man who could say "I'm sorry," a man who would forgive me, too. For all of that and more, I had chosen him.

Now, Dad held the hand and waist of Mrs. Brandon Wells as we danced. Far in the past, a little girl crawled across his chest and stole his John Deere cap, blue eyes grinning into the face of the camera. She asked for Hooper Humperdink at bedtime again, and now we can all recite it from memory—*Pinky, Pat and Pasternack, I bet they come by camel back!* Back there, too, she watched her mom and dad spin slowly in the living room to "If We Make It Through December," not knowing then the depth in that melody, not knowing then the weight behind eyes connecting and smiles, what it means to make it through December, together. He taught that little girl the cast of a rod, the slow click and reel after the bobber plunked onto the surface of the water, how to bait a hook with a squirming nightcrawler. He coached the in-and-out of orange construction cones for hours until she mastered how to parallel park before her final driving test. Whether intentionally or accidentally, he had been preparing me.

Now, we turned slow around the dance floor, each sway a step closer to the last note in the song. Gone was the night we stared up at the cloudless sky on the hill by the old maple and waited for the meteor shower. Evenings swaying in front of a fire pit, turning front ways then back to warm our bodies as we talked about God and faith and family and regret, until the coals flashed red and black, flames dying, then walking slowly into the house to bed. There would be no more creasing wrapping paper in the dry heat of the excavator's shop on Christmas Eve with him, no more Dad topping off and lifting my bushel basket of corn from the end of a row and spilling it with ease into the bed of the red pickup truck, Dad gunning the accelerator of the snowmobile through the fields with me clinging to his coat toasty in my snowsuit and helmet, Dad showing me the slow slide of a cue stick between thumb and index finger and then the thrust that sent the cue ball breaking against the racked triangle of billiard balls.

All of life before that day squeezed between his dusty calloused hands and mine, a slow turning, slow turning until the end notes began to play. Even over the black tuxedo, fresh trim and aftershave, I could breathe him in when we embraced, the scent of sweat and sun and earth and oil.

"I love you, Sare," he said.

"I love you, too, Dad."

"It is a beautiful song," Mom tells me later, "and we chose it for a beautiful girl." Maybe it *was* perfect. As Mickey Gilley lulled a final line, Dad spun me out, then pulled me back in, my white dress billowing, the bill of his Father-of-the-Bride cap shadowing his smile.

Telling My Daughter Love Stories

I TELL MY DAUGHTER love stories, some I've made up and others that are true, from fairy tales and novels I read once, grandparents who grew up across the street from one another, the boys I dated in and after high school, the man I finally married. She is giddy and attentive in the back seat of the car and we share smiles and make eye contact in the rear-view mirror as I drive. I draw out each tale to ramp up the suspense—will they get together? will they live happily ever after?—until finally, "And then," pause, "they lived happily ever after!"

They aren't all happily ever after stories. Lydia is seven, and I just can't bring myself to end, "and they went their separate ways," the reality of love faded, over, broken, not enough; it seems too much for a dreamer like my daughter to bear. Instead, after I weave the star-crossed tale of a country girl (me) and a Parrothead (Eric), I say, "and then they went on to find other people to spend their lives with." It's mostly true. I know Eric married in North Carolina. I know he divorced shortly thereafter and moved back to our hometown. Was he married now? Did he have children of his own? Would I run into him at the gas station on the corner of East Washington and Bainbridge Road the next time I went home to my parents' house? These questions roll along with me as I drive. What has happened to the man I loved obsessively for two short years? Is he happy with the choices he has made? Has he found a happily ever after?

I don't share any of that with Lydia, though. Like most girls I know, Lydia's favorite ending is happily ever after. Who doesn't love a good love scene, a not-yet couple waiting for each other in a city garden while "Somewhere Over the Rainbow" plays, Tom Hanks chasing his dog and then they meet, "Don't cry, Shopgirl, don't cry," and Meg Ryan says, "I wanted it to be you. I wanted it to be you so bad," then the timid lean in by Tom Hanks to the most gentle of kisses, then the arms move in slow motion around neck and waist to a full on body embrace, and of course there's the dog so obediently trained to stand next to his master and bark with enthusiasm about this first kiss as the camera zooms out, the garden green and alive, Meg and Tom perfectly positioned with the fountain in the lens. Everything is centered, this is it, the wooing and wondering are over. "I wanted it to be you," Meg Ryan says. Love. Kiss. Happily ever after.

Yes, Meg, it's him! It's him! I sob and laugh and sob.

I can watch *You've Got Mail* and *When Harry Met Sally* and *Forget Paris* and a million other romantic comedies over and over again and I will always cry along with Shopgirl, hug my pillow and my glass of wine. Leading actresses who are with the wrong guy, leading actors who are with the wrong girl, leading actors and actresses who discover by the end of the movie that they love each other, actually, that the first relationship was good, sure, good enough in fact that most of the time the couples were ready to commit to a lifetime together, but now, well, it either wasn't great, or it wasn't great enough or someone messed it up or now, wow, this other person! They touch the circuits that weren't triggered with the first, their compatibility is so much better than anything ever anticipated or experienced, *this* is what they've been waiting for. No more messing around with a ratchet set, trying to adjust the wheel of a wrench until it fits. This one is it.

I'm crazy about these movies, these predictable yet entertaining comedies I can laugh at and cry through, and it isn't because Meg Ryan is just the darned cutest person who ever starred in an eighties or nineties romantic comedy, it isn't because of Hugh Grant's bloodhound eyes and British accent. These stories are magical. Romantic. They capture a singular moment in time when two strangers met and fell in love.

There wasn't anything particularly magical about the way that Brandon and I met, though if I work at it, I can twist it into this serendipitous event that launched us into the life we were meant to live, how he had just moved back from Texas, how I had finally decided I was okay being single (and isn't that the way it always goes?), how we were both visiting the mega-church where we met, a tiny chance encounter at a barbecue, and would you look at where that's taken us, so far, eleven years later and three children. Just like that, it's magic. Scripted. Special. Blessed. And therefore, protected. Untouchable. Indestructible.

❊

I gripped a red Solo cup between my hands and smiled, looking hopefully about the kitchen and living area. People everywhere were engaged in lively conversations, laughing and chattering. I was backed into the corner of a dimly lit kitchen by a gnome-ish English major at the church "college and career" barbecue. Help me. Please. Gnome-ish English major hovered and swayed dangerously, his broad frame blocking any possible exit. He wielded the plot of his novel-in-progress, swaying forward and backward, the plot's one endless sentence like a dramatic ribbon spinning and dancing through the air. I smiled more and nodded. Please. Help me. Anybody.

Suddenly, there he was, a quick-witted, sarcastic knight in Adidas shoes, interjecting a line we laughed at together, a solid hook that reeled me away. The gnome-ish English major stayed in the corner. From where I stood, I could see him slouching, swaying, frowning.

I watched my rescuer as he talked. Who was this man? He had a lively laugh, loud voice, kind eyes, an athletic build, and a sarcastic sense of humor. He wore a polo shirt tucked into khaki shorts with a belt. He was clean-cut, a high school teacher, an athletic director, a coach. We listed our top five favorite movies and quoted from *Dumb and Dumber*—"Our pets' heads are falling off!" He not only listened to country music but also frequented a country line dance bar in Akron. I didn't really catch his name when he introduced himself, and everyone around called him by his last name, "Wells" or "Wellsy" or "B-dubs," never his actual, real first name, but I knew it had a "B" in it. Brian? Bradley?

I left the party without his number. We laughed a lot. I liked his eyes. He was there again with his friend, Chris, at the College and Career Sunday school class the next weekend and we sat together. The two of them called each other by their last names, "Wells" and "Love."

"Hey, Love," Brian said, "What do you want to do for lunch?"

I wanted to invite myself along. After church, I walked slowly through the sanctuary, keeping an eye out for him, and then began to mosey toward my car. *Oh, forget it, stop chasing,* I thought with a smile. My heels clicked smartly against the pavement, the hem of my skirt swished against my knees. I watched the horizon instead of the asphalt in front of me. As I reached my car, I heard the slap of running feet against the parking lot, a "Hey!" and turned to see Bradley sprinting towards me. "Do you want to go to lunch?"

Brian or Bradley carried John Grisham's *The Testament* with him to lunch. *Oh, he reads!* I thought. He loved God, *Dumb and Dumber*, country music, and books. It was so much easier already, so fewer issues to compromise on or to convert him into tolerating. I flirted and chatted throughout lunch at Panera, wit and banter smooth and easy with him, natural. We made plans to meet up at the Boot Scoot'n Saloon that Wednesday and exchanged numbers.

It was dark and loud and crowded but he was nearby, a line in front or right behind, always within sight. When the dance turned ninety degrees and he was in front of me, I watched him kick his cowboy boots, twist his waist in dark blue jeans, and shake his head in a black cowboy hat. I forgot the next steps and stared at his feet or whatever pair of feet moved in front of me next until I could pick up the grapevine, the rock step, the kick and stomp and hip swivel. He led me in a waltz, his arms commanding as I giggled and listened for his cues, his eyes locked to mine, determined. During a slow dance his voice was loud and strong in my ear. He had a liquid gold sound and I felt it through his breath on my neck, his cologne in my nose and I breathed deep, closed my eyes and smiled. It was warm there in his grip.

I felt his eyes on me during "Steam" and I tried to be sexy, slinked along the grapevine, dipped and strutted and swayed. Ten years later, we'll dance tipsy in our kitchen to whatever plays on the radio and he'll laugh as I dip and strut and sway, because no matter how I try, sexy doesn't fit on me, and I feel silly gyrating hips, shimmying my chest, shaking my ass. We'll laugh and keep dancing, and then he'll pull me close and kiss me long, and we'll slow dance to John Hiatt before whispering, *Let's go upstairs*, because it doesn't matter how I shake it, he still loves it.

When the night was over, he walked me to my car, a tight hug, hands squeezed, a peck on the lips, but no more. I tried to wait to call, waited all day Thursday and all day Friday but by Saturday afternoon I couldn't help myself. Like an overeager teenager, I called and got his voice mail, hung up and dialed again, listened over and over as his message said, "Hi, this is Br . . . Wells, I can't come to the phone right now so leave a message," Br . . . ? Bradley? Brian?

Finally I left a message, "Hi! It's Sarah. I'm just calling to see if you'd want to come play softball with my church softball team this Sunday, so give me a call when you get this, okay? Okay, talk to you later, bye!"

I wanted to be pursued. I wanted to fall in love and stay in love as if it's a terminal disease you can't help but catch, as if love just happens to you. I wanted to live a romantic comedy, to find the one person in this world meant for me, one prince I was shaped and formed to complete.

But that isn't true. No matter what size, there's probably a whole brand of wrenches that fits your screw.

The truth is Brandon was engaged before we met. The truth is I would have married Eric, if he had asked me. The truth is we probably would have made it work with the people we loved before, whether they were good mates or great mates or not the best match, but okay, here we are, vowed. The truth is married love isn't magic.

When we watch the Disney princesses, Lydia, too, is programmed for this romance. She *loves* love, she says.

"They're getting in love, aren't they, mama?" she says. Getting in love. I like this better than falling. Getting is becoming, growing, receiving, changing, realizing, acquiring; it is an active pursuit of some object. It is intentional.

These stories about true love, one and only love, soulmate love, *Poof!* love are incomplete. I don't want to set my daughter up for disappointment or leave her underprepared for the kind of commitment it takes to marry someone and make it stick. I also don't want to terrify her into nunnery, or drive her into love too young, or cause her to over-rationalize love, but especially, I don't want her to make the same mistakes I did, which is of course what every parent thinks. How can I spare my child from the self-inflicted grief and injustices endured, how can I prepare her for the real world, be present for her in the first love and in the first brokenness, help her to navigate relationships?

My husband is a darn good wrench to my screw. Brandon and I debated and considered whether it was "God's will" for us to be together. We read our arguments and conversations like tarot cards to determine whether God was blessing this relationship or condemning it. But what is God's will, except to love, to be whole, to worship in spirit and in truth? How with our own free will shall we live in God's will? Whom should we choose as a mate, except one who will also choose to walk in love, to pursue wholeness, to worship in spirit and in truth?

My father walked me down the aisle to Pachelbel's "Canon in D," his arm tight around mine, and gave me over to be wed in the church where I was baptized earlier that spring, by the pastor who baptized each of us. We said "I do" surrounded by ten groomsmen and six bridesmaids and then knelt for communion. We listened to my friend, Pauli, sing Garth Brooks's "You Move Me" and our friend, Kate Tucker, sing Third Day's "Love Song," and then we glided out of the sanctuary lifting praises to Jesus along with the "Victory Chant." We hugged people we mostly knew and some we didn't at all, posed plastic for photo after photo, and rode in the surprise limo to the reception barn. My aunts and grandma played folk music on the piano, accordion, and guitar on the porch in the September sun, and we greeted hundreds of guests and cut cake. Brandon and I danced to Marc Cohn's "True Companion," Dad lead me around to "True Love Ways," my mother-in-law rocked it out with Brandon to "Mambo No. 5," and Wellsy and Love line danced to "Good Brown Gravy." Brandon removed my garter to The Rolling Stones and we grinned at each other, promising never to be each other's beast of burden, and we line danced to "YMCA" and spun in circles and tossed my bouquet, and then, so tired, we stood at the door of the barn and waved, a goodbye wave like Pop who passed away before I knew him, waved to the camera at the door to the barn and left the party still going, the party that required three additional beer runs to the local drive thru to restock the bar. After we waved goodbye and hugged our parents and thanked them over and over, we rode in the butter-covered truck to Walden and a honeymoon suite paid for by his parents, and we kicked off our shoes and unzipped my dress, and we slid into a bubble bath with rose petals and champagne and Brandon picked the bobby pins out of my hair, so many bobby pins, and after all of that, we crawled into bed and made love, free from guilt and held by vows.

That wasn't happily ever after, either. Just "to be continued."

The story line continues, Princess. Thank God it continues. It continued past starry eyed adoration and *Yes! Yes! I love you! I do!*, into the hours of ennui in the evenings as he played general manager of his fictitious video game baseball team and I grumbled in the kitchen over a frozen pizza and dirty dishes. It continued after the wedding gifts were slipped into the cabinets and I had to actually start cooking. It continues and evolves, it is molded and melted and formed and fractured and healed.

We were not made for each other; we are constantly making room for each other, sometimes collide or ricochet off each other but we have decided to share this space, grow together in this space, and protect this space when it's under threat. The happily ever after is forever in-progress.

I tell Lydia another story, and another and another and another, and each one goes like this: The boy and the girl meet in a strange and random way they will later call serendipitous, they go to the movies and take long walks and talk for hours, they are both present in the same moment of time, aligned in their tastes or interests or values, and love catches them by surprise like a sudden gust of wind or a blast of sun through the trees. And then, a series of small and unremarkable conflicts happen, and those two people grow up and change, and then they look at each other and all that they've been through so far, how far apart they've grown, how near they still are to one another, what they have built between them, and they must decide. How do we keep growing up and changing together? Can we?

Recently I've noticed a new trend in romantic comedies: it's the marriage-under-fire. Unlike the romantic comedies of the late eighties and early nineties, these newer shows, like *Marriage Retreat*, *Spanglish*, *I Don't Know How She Does It*, and *Date Night* strike a different chord. Here, marriage has fallen into its routine and ritual. The ennui of the day-to-day maintenance becomes a slow, unnoticeable descent into survival. Survival is interrupted by distractions, diversions, and danger, all jolts to the stagnant marriages that force closer analysis and relationship-changing decisions. In the dark of our living room, Brandon and I sit together on the couch, a noticeable gap between our bodies, and watch these flicks, feeling as uncomfortable as if we were watching a hot sex scene with our parents in the room.

I don't like being able to relate so closely to these movies, their minor and major distractions and temptations, their simple and complex speed bumps and stumbling blocks, their basic and advanced challenges and choices. But here we are, married with all of these things, facing the choice daily to be selfless or selfish, to concede or to stand firm on our position, to yell or speak or keep silent, to indulge or entertain or run as fast as we can away from temptations and back into the waiting and hopefully merciful arms of each other.

This is all a smidgen premature. Lydia is seven. She isn't interested in boys, although they are already chasing her around the playground. She can't watch these romantic comedies with me, yet, though in good time, we will snuggle on the couch sharing a bowlful of popcorn and sob. It is the princess she cares about now—royalty, beauty, grace, kindness, bravery. She celebrates these characters in stickers, coloring books, and movies. Cinderella, Snow White, Sleeping Beauty, and Rapunzel, all rescued from evil by the good prince and swept away into a happily ever after. I am glad her every neuron isn't trained on men, oh, thank God, at seven she isn't already planning her wedding, crooning over a boy in her class. She talks about wanting to marry someone, someday, in the same narrative as wanting to be a teacher or a gymnast or a swimmer or an artist.

It is this part of the story I've neglected. Buried under my pursuit of love, my rush to secure some happily ever after is the fear that Lydia will leave behind her own identity and latch onto a man's, finding love before she's found herself. *It doesn't have to be that way*, I want to say. You can be and should be a whole person yourself. Forget the love stories for a moment and focus only on your beauty, your spirit, your brilliance, your strength, your value. You, my darling, are the glory of God, all on your own. You have been made with a purpose beyond leaving and cleaving, beyond completing some other person. If it should happen that you find a companion who is also a whole person to share your life with, wonderful. Know yourself. Know him. This familiarity and intimacy will become security, rest, ease, trust, faith. Love. Make room for each other to grow, shift, and change.

Know, however, that it will *not* be happily ever after. It will be hard and lovely and frustrating and joyful and grievous and beautiful and painful and holy. And it will be worth every moment, worth every right turn and mercy extended and forgiveness given.

In the kitchen, Brandon washes and dries dishes to the tune of sports talk radio. The kids are launching their bodies over the couches and onto pillows in the living room, like they aren't supposed to do, giggling and tackling, tickling and squealing and then crying because, inevitably, one of them gets hurt.

"Hey!" he growls over his shoulder, "Enough!"

I walk into the kitchen still in my work clothes, the last email exchange and business matter still clinging like static in my brain, the hope to pursue a writing idea after the kids go to bed eager to become reality, but right now, I am Mom. I am Wife. And I am home, home to waltz around the kitchen making dinner with him, home to fold some clothes, home to wash some bodies and read some books, home to fold my arms around his waist, rest my head on his shoulder, squeeze.

He pulls the dry towel off his shoulder, throws it on the counter, drops the wet towel into the sink of dishes, and turns around, hands on my waist. I reach up to kiss his forehead, run my fingers through his hair, and smile into his eyes, kiss his cheeks and his earlobe and his neck until the tension shivers off him. He lifts his hands to my face, turns my lips to his, and we kiss, a soft, yearning kiss. His jaw clenches and he squeezes my waist again, swats my rear end.

"Kids," he teases, "Bedtime!" It's only five o'clock. Elvis runs through for the basement and Legos. Henry marches in to stand on my toes and beg for juice. Lydia hovers in the doorway of the kitchen, watching us be more than Mom and Dad for a moment, glimpses us as husband and wife.

And then, there it is, right in front of me. I do not need to tell Lydia these love stories. I do not need to lecture her on the nature of love, on romantic attraction, on the type of man to marry, on how to build a sustainable marriage, on how to survive financial crises, miscarriage, infertility, grief, disagreements, moves, career changes, raising children, or temptation. I just need to live out a love story rooted in the things I believe in—grace, mercy, forgiveness—with my husband, with her father, and let her watch this romantic comedy.

Just that. That's all.

Careful Intimacies

I WEAR MY TALL brown boots and short white dress and walk with you like we haven't been married over a decade and don't have three children. They are at your parents' house, baking ginger cookies and picking daffodils and dandelions, for me, because they're sweet.

We will not talk about the kids tonight, not because we do not love them, but precisely because we love them.

"Just imagine, in four years," you say, "we could tell Lydia we'll be back in a few hours and just . . . leave." I try to imagine it and can't.

We talk about anything except upcoming coach-pitch practice, Cub Scouts, and gymnastics. We order two sides and a couple of drinks at The Lockview. It's our kind of crowd, our kind of bar, hipster, and you secretly love hipster-ish things.

"I can't pull off hipster," you say.

"Yeah, skinny jeans don't work for you," I say.

"No way, but if big-ass-baggy-short-white-guy jeans were popular, I'd be in."

"We could market that," I say, "It has a nice ring to it." We drink and people-watch. That guy diagonal from us, he could be my grandpa's cousin. "Maybe he *is* my grandpa's cousin," I say.

Grandpa's been dead for over seven years. Our middle son, Elvis, was four months old when I sat alone next to Grandpa's hospice bed and prayed for him to give up his spirit while Mom and Grandma rested, my skin prickling as he sighed one last time and I half-spoke and whispered, "Brandon? I think he's gone."

You came in quick with Elvis in your arms, our tiny cranky infant who nearly died just four months earlier because he couldn't breathe as he exited my interior, capillaries sticky and stubborn.

But we're not talking about them now, because the sun is shining and it's just us this evening, just us and your Old Fashioned, my Lemon Ice martini. I am determined to take as many selfies with you as you do with the guys when you're on the road for work. I tag it on Facebook, "Bold and the Beautiful?" and you say, "You mean *bald* and the beautiful," because it's been almost twelve years since we married and you feel bald and old, though you are neither. It doesn't matter because you feel it, my Mr. Smooth who walks slowly sometimes, suave through his back pain, knee pain, elbow pain. Mr. Smooth's hairline is receding but come on, husband, I don't notice. You grew out your goatee again, and I love you with a goatee, its bristles against my chin when we kiss.

This is the second time we're seeing Lyle Lovett and the third for John Hiatt. You raise your drink and toast, "Happy Valentine's Day!" these tickets a gift from me to you. One Valentine's Day, we saw a Christian rock group and the next we spent in the hospital for a follow-up miscarriage procedure. It's April 26 and the second time we've been out together this month, with so many road trips and conferences, gymnastics and softball practices.

I have my hand on your thigh and your hand covers mine. Our knees are touching in orchestra row J, seats three and four, and we are keeping time to the beat with our touching knees. John Hiatt finishes singing, "Marlene," and Lyle Lovett says something to John Hiatt about his songwriting, how he knows Mrs. Hiatt and Mrs. Hiatt's name isn't Marlene. Hiatt has been married twenty-nine years. I squeeze Brandon's hand. I try to imagine life in another seventeen years.

The guy in front of us passed out and hasn't moved for at least an hour. You lean in close and whisper-yell how that happened to you once at a Merle Haggard concert, back when you were dating Devin, maybe? We call that "BS," before Sarah. The guy in front of us will have a crick in his neck when he wakes up. He still isn't waking up, even as Lyle Lovett sings, "My Baby Don't Tolerate."

❋

Twenty-four hours ago, you asked, "Do you mind if I go play golf with Jerry?"

I stuffed one sock inside the other as I folded laundry and said, "No problem. Do you know when you'll be back?"

You smiled with your golf gear in your arms and said, "I don't know." I grabbed a shirt and folded it the way my mom taught me.

"Well, are you going to play nine holes or eighteen, are you going to eat dinner together? Do you think you'll go to sing karaoke after?" I replied, the way my mom never replied.

You laughed. "I just don't know, okay?"

I dropped a pair of Henry's underwear into the stack of Minion-printed briefs, the way you prefer because it's stupid to fold boys' underwear. It's *underwear*, you say.

"Well," I said, "I think it's only fair to give *some* clue as to when you will be home—it's not that I care, I don't," I lied, trying to negotiate the same space as usual, quality time and childcare and your priorities and my neediness, "I just want to know so I know whether to be excited you'll be home soon at eight or to settle into an evening of reading, knowing you'll be back after I'm in bed. Either way is fine. I just want to know."

"I don't like these kinds of restraints," you said, and I started to say, "Then maybe you shouldn't have gotten married."

As the words fell out, I remembered our confessions just a week earlier, my blubbering, "Why can't you just say you think I'm pretty?" at the most intimate moment, when things weren't working in harmony, in that fragile space.

You rolled off of me and sobbed, "You make me feel like such a failure!" How we held each other, how we apologized, how we touched each other's faces and whispered all our truths into old wounds.

I remember this as the words drip, *Maybe you shouldn't have gotten married.*

When we hit an impasse, you angry and calling off golf, me angry and finishing folding laundry, I carried our daughter's clothes back to her bedroom to find her with her friend tucked behind the door.

"What are you doing?" I asked, reading their guilt.

"Nothing," they said.

"You can leave those on my bed, I'll put them away," Lydia said and left.

I wondered what she overheard, what she was listening for in between our living room remarks. I thought back to my own ear against the door eavesdropping on my parents as my dad yelled his frustration in the dark of night. "You never . . . " he said, my ears too young to hear or know what she never did but old enough to know my mom was crying and lying in bed, my dad standing somewhere in the dark bedroom. I wondered if they might divorce, maybe even cried into my pillow and prayed before drifting off to sleep.

"She said they weren't listening to us," you told me when I returned to the living room. "'We didn't hear one word you said,' she said." We rolled our eyes and smiled thin lines. You went out to the front of the house and I went out to the back of the house. Later, we would lean close into each other in our bedroom and forget, but until then, you shot hoops and I cut shrubs all afternoon, one of each of our children by our sides, separate.

But we're not talking about them now, or that. Like love keeps no record of wrongs, it took me a long time to remember exactly what it was Lydia and her friend might have overheard just yesterday, and now that I have I've remembered, too, a long list of other wrongs dealt and received. I flinch a little because now John Hiatt is singing about how long he's loved his girl in "Have a Little Faith in Me," and your fingers are interlaced with mine. This is the song you burned onto that CD you made me a month after we met, along with a dozen others I remember.

I remember it all again in a moment, it's all here, Grandpa and my parents and your parents and our exes, our vices, our joys, all of it is here between us now, held in between our interlaced fingers.

Okay, so our love keeps record of wrongs, but also mercies. After all, we are here. We hold our wrongs and mercies together in careful intimacy. I run my fingernails across the grooves in your big-ass-baggy-short-white-guy jeans and you put your hand on my knee, just below my dress's white hemline.

At any moment, I think John Hiatt's voice might splinter and that'll be it, but he just keeps hanging on to those notes, he just keeps singing, *Please! Please! Please, now baby!* By the time the concert is over, the drunk man in front of us is up and clapping. It's only 9:16 p.m.—you guessed 9:15 p.m. and I guessed 9:30 p.m., so you win. We want them to play more, longer, but they are finished.

We slip out the side exit, your fingers grazing the small of my back as we walk through the sheep-shuffle of concertgoers.

"Want to get a drink and a bite in the Valley?" you ask, even though it's Sunday and I have to get up for work tomorrow, you have to take our children to school. We are not tired, and our children might not even be asleep yet.

Let's stay away a little while longer, darling.

Notes, Extras, and Small Mercies

Field Guide to Resisting Temptation
"Field Guide. . . " was published online at *Brevity* magazine the day that Brandon went to sing karaoke in "Not-My-Husband."

Rules of Engagement
The Macaroni Grille we ate at the day I graduated and the night Brandon proposed had a fire in their kitchen and closed a couple of years later.

Buck Owens Teaches Me about Listening
Parts of this chapter incorporate bits from another essay, "Country Boys, City Boys," which originally appeared in *River Teeth: A Journal of Nonfiction Narrative*, and was listed as a Notable Essay in *Best American Essays*. Dolly Surprise had hair that miraculously grew three inches from her ponytail when you raised her right arm. My gratitude to Chevy Chase and the movie *Vegas Vacation* for inspiring my father's dam jokes.

Building Fires
"Lord, lead us not into temptation but deliver us from evil" is from Matt 6:13 NIV. The engine of the truck we cosigned on blew up the week we got married. The restaurant Brandon and I went to for our first date was called Timberfire and burnt to the ground shortly after we got married. My preferred breakup reading was the *Mark of the Lion* trilogy by Francine Rivers. The Malachi passage is from Mal 3:10 NIV. "I have loved you with an everlasting love; I have drawn you with unfailing kindness" is from Jer 31:3 NIV.

Uprooted
My grandma, Jean, passed down the family stories of Oliver and Catherine Davis, verified through census records and entries on Ancestry.com. History of farm life in the 1800s was acquired from an editorial in *The New York Times*, "Our Farm Life in 1840," by Warner Miller of New York, November 24, 1916.

The Seeds You Sow
"Seed Trouble" is the *Curious George* episode Henry and I watched before I left for work.

Somebody's Daughter
The introduction of this chapter is adapted from my poem, "Sunday Worship," which appeared in *Pruning Burning Bushes*. Thanks to Wikipedia for the demographic data on Auburn.

Genotype
That one actor that plays that blind guy in that one movie is Al Pacino, and he plays a blind guy in *Scent of a Woman*.

Someone's in the Kitchen
"Dripping faucet of a wife" is a reference to Proverbs 27:15-16 MSG, "A nagging spouse is like the drip, drip, drip of a leaky faucet; You can't turn it off, and you can't get away from it."

The Worst Soccer Mom
Tuffy the Eagle is the mascot of Ashland University, the school where I worked.

Friends in Low Places
"There's a Tear in My Beer" is a Hank Williams song, sung by both Hank Williams Sr. and Hank Williams Jr., who wrote and sang a song called "Family Tradition." "Froggy Went a Courtin'" was recorded by Tex Ritter.

I Take to Drinking
Pickle Bill's is a casual seafood restaurant near the shore of Lake Erie. "Do not get drunk on wine, which leads to debauchery. Instead, be filled with the Spirit, speaking to one another with psalms, hymns, and songs from the Spirit. Sing and make music from your heart to the Lord, always giving thanks to God the Father for everything, in the name of our Lord Jesus Christ" is from Eph 5:18-20 NIV. "Go, eat your food with gladness, and

drink wine with a joyful heart, for God has already approved of what you do" is from Eccl 9:7 NIV.

The Face of Mercy
The title of this essay is a loose nod to Jo Ann Beard's essay, "The Fourth State of Matter" in her book, *The Boys of My Youth*. In the essay, Beard refers to her dog as "the face of love." Parts of this chapter are adapted from "The Bride of Christ," an essay that previously appeared in *The Cresset*.

The First Step Is Admitting You Have a Problem
"Life of contentment" in Ecclesiastes is a reference to "Enjoy life with your wife, whom you love, all the days of this meaningless life that God has given you under the sun—all your meaningless days. For this is your lot in life and in your toilsome labor under the sun," Eccl 9:9 NIV.

Not-My-Husband
The pet name "Tiny Dancer" is from the Elton John song by the same name. The Joseph and Potiphar's wife story is from Gen 39.

He Thinks He'll Keep Her
The ruby poem was originally published by Tiffany and Co. "Two are better than one, because they have a good return for their labor: If either of them falls down, one can help the other up. But pity anyone who falls and has no one to help them up. Though one may be overpowered, two can defend themselves. A cord of three strands is not quickly broken" is from Eccl 4:9–10,12. "Love is patient, love is kind, love never fails," are references to 1 Cor 13.

The Dance: Dad's Lead
Hooper Humperdink, Not Him! is a book by Dr. Seuss.

Telling My Daughter Love Stories
The "happily ever after" scene with Tom Hanks and Meg Ryan is from *You've Got Mail*. To "worship in spirit and truth" is from John 4:24 NIV.

Careful Intimacies
"Love keeps no record of wrongs" references 1 Cor 13.

Made in the USA
Monee, IL
15 December 2021

85466686R00105